Returning to the Abbey of the Holy Ghost

Chris Wickland

Returning to the abbey of the Holy Ghost

Copyright 2021 by Christopher Wickland

Published by Amazon

All Rights reserved. No part of this publication may be reproduced, stored in a retrieval system, or transmitted in any form by any means, electronic, mechanical, photocopy, recording, or otherwise, without the prior permission of the author.

Cover photo by Chris Wickland

Cover design by Christopher Wickland

First printing 2021

Scripture quotations marked ESV are from the ESV bible (The Holy Bible, English Standard Version), copyright 2001 by Crossway Bibles, a publishing ministry of Good News Publishers. Used by Permission. All rights reserved.

Scripture quotations marked KJV are taken from the King James Version of the Bible.

Scripture quotations marked Douay Rheims are taken from the Douay Rheims bible.

Scripture references marked NIV are from The Holy Bible: New International Version. Copyright 1973, 1978, 1984 by International Bible Society. Zondervan Publishing House. Used by Permission. All rights reserved.

Scripture references marked NRSV are from the New Revised Standard Version Bible, copyright 1989, Division of Christian Education of the National Council of Churches of Christ in the U.S.A Used by Permission. All rights reserved.

Scripture references marked NASB taken from the NEW AMERICAN STANDARD BIBLE, Copyright 1960, 1962, 1968, 1971, 1972, 1973, 1975, 1977, 1995 by the Lockman Foundation. Used by Permission. All rights reserved.

Scripture quotations marked JB are taken from the Jerusalem Bible.

Scripture references marked NABRE are taken from the New American Bible Revised Edition, copyright 2010,1991,1986, 1970.

All emphasis in Scripture quotations have been added by the author.

Dedication

This book is dedicated to the nuns at Park Place Pastoral Centre, Wickham, and to the monks at Quarr Abbey on the Isle of Wight.

Contents

Introduction
Layout of a typical abbey
1. All may find this abbey in their soul
2. The Holy Spirit, good walls and the four ladies
3. Obedience, mercy, patience and strength
4. The house founded upon seven pillars, that Lady Wisdom built
5. The cloister of the abbey and the structure of the abbey's offices
6. Construct the convent and let God the Father, Son and Holy Ghost build it
7. Lady Charity must be abbess of our abbey of the Holy Ghost
8. Madame Wisdom must be the prioress and Lady Humility the sub prioress of the abbey of the Holy Ghost
9. Jesus Christ demonstrated in many ways His great love for us by His incarnation, His passion and His cruel death
10. We must recognise the great love our Lord Jesus Christ has toward us
11. By the authority of the blessed Trinity, all grace and kindness comes from Him
12. How one might anger the Lord by being unkind toward the poor
13. No person should counterfeit more beauty than nature permitted
14. The way of self examination, sufferings and praises
15. Climb the mountain of tranquility
16. The duties of Discretion, Praise, Devotion and Penitence in our abbey of the Holy Ghost
17. Jesus promises abundance to those who serve Him well.
18. We must guard our hearts with all diligence in the love of our Lord
19. Watch out for the evil sisters, Envy, Pride, Murmer and False Judgement
20. It is by prayer that the four daughters of Satan will be removed from the abbey of the Holy Ghost
21. Conclusion to Returning to the abbey of the Holy Ghost

Introduction

In mid May of 1992, I found myself suddenly out of a job due to my own stupidity and stubbornness. My landlord made it very clear to me that I had to go to the Job Centre and get a job forthwith. As I looked in the window at the various array of jobs I clearly could not do, I suddenly spotted a cleaning job at a convent called 'Park Place,' in Wickham, Hampshire. So I applied for the position, got an interview and began work the following day.

What took place over the next eight months changed my life forever. I was 19 years of age at the time and sadly I really didn't appreciate what had been handed to me, it was providence from God Himself. I wasn't particularly that keen on the job and only in hindsight do I now appreciate the special and priceless gift of time I had at that convent.

Most people very rarely get to see a nun, let alone spend time with one. Yet because of the nature of my job, I spent about quarter of my day in the presence of some godly, beautiful Franciscan nuns.

They were a wonderful community of ladies who worked hard running a conference centre as well as being devoted in prayer to their husband Jesus.

In spending time with these nuns I got to see faith and piety in action in the context of community. I was privileged to see upfront and personal the lives of those nuns and how devoted they were to their calling and to one another. To this day, I have to be honest and say I have never quite experienced in Christendom what I experienced at Park Place.

Spending time with these nuns, I asked if they would teach me how to pray. They were always willing to spend some moments of time with me each day to teach me about contemplative prayer. At the time some of the things they taught me seemed strange to my little Protestant ears. However, I soon began to see the wisdom of what they taught.

Before long I was spending my lunch hours in the main chapel devoted to prayer. God in His goodness toward my yearning heart encouraged me greatly in contemplative prayer with His presence. There were times where His presence was so strong that I really didn't know how to cope with it. This effected me so much that I think my Protestant Christian friends were becoming concerned about how much it was changing me.

It was here to my shame where things sadly took a sharp left turn. As people were concerned about my deep prayer life and how it was changing me, they started giving me strong anti Catholic literature to read. I was so shocked that I felt I couldn't really continue at the covenant and so left and avoided everything Catholic for the next 25 years. For this, I am now deeply ashamed and sorry.

In 2019 my family all went on a week holiday to the Isle of Wight. As we were traveling over the water on the local ferry I saw an advertisement for a monastery called Quarr Abbey. As soon as I saw it, I felt like a man possessed. I knew I had to go there and I had to get there immediately. My wife kindly acquiesced and later that day we visited the Abbey.

As soon as I crossed the threshold into the Abbey something hit my chest, it was like a fire and a burden all in one, which chose to sit and reside, burning away in my heart. At first I really didn't understand what this was. However, later in the week it became clear what this burning fire in my chest was. I will explain more later.

Inside the Abbey they had a bookstore which I was desperate to peruse. As I came into the the store I felt as though I were transported to another world. It was Christianity but from a perspective I had never seen before.

There were books by various saints such as Saint Teresa of Avila and a whole load of wonders written long before the reformation. I was stunned, shocked and saddened all in one hit. How was it that I had assumed that church history only began 500 years ago with the likes of Luther and Calvin? Here in this little book shop was a treasure trove of wonders that I knew I had to avail myself of.

That day began the unravelling of my prejudices and misunderstandings. As I read books about famous nuns and monks from long before the Reformation, I quickly realised that as a Protestant I was somewhat devoid and divorced from a history which was mine by birth right.

On the last day of my holiday on the Isle of Wight, I had an experience which I could only call a night of wrestling with God. The fire which hit me when I entered Quarr abbey several days previously wouldn't leave me. It just burned and burned. I could barely think straight or sleep. It just burned and burned. God was opening my eyes to the treasure and richness of the church and I needed to know these treasures and embrace them. It was time to put away my misinformed prejudices and open my eyes to the vast riches from church history.

Since that time, I have been on a wonderful journey of enrichment and much study and practice in the art of prayer, thanks to old ancient books written by Catholic and Orthodox monks and nuns. They have left a wonderful depository of knowledge and disciplines that can teach us how to walk closer to God and have a more meaningful and richer experience of God's presence that will fundamentally change us.

The holiness, piety, closeness to God that I always desired was to be found not in the Protestant literature, but in Catholic and Orthodox spirituality. This is not to say that there are not great books written by Protestants based on meditation and contemplative prayer. However, many of those books themselves have been influenced by the teachings and disciplines which come from Catholic and Orthodox spirituality.

Now that you know a little of my story, I need to explain the title of this book. 'Returning to the Abbey of the Holy Ghost.'

There was an interesting and famous small book written in the middle ages titled, 'The Abbey of the Holy Ghost.' It is a little treatise written around 1350 - 1375 on how to live the spiritual life without having to become a monk or a nun. It is a teaching manual that helps to develop a metaphorical monastic abbey in the heart of the Christian, to enable them to live a more contemplative, spiritual life in the every day world.

I have a copy of this wonderful little book, yet for today's reader it may seem somewhat odd and alien to our culture. In its day, it was a 'must read' for many a lay person. The knowledge and language it contained did not need to be practically explained, as it was already understood by the people of the day. However, in today's world we are sadly removed from a society that was run and governed by the church. We live in a secular world and such pious and religious language needs to be reinterpreted and explained for today's reader.

I deemed it would be good to take the basic structure of that ancient book and add some flesh and bones to it so that the modern reader may more readily and practically understand it. Of course I am no monk or nun, but I have spent the last few years living a life based on monastic teachings and have learned so much already.

I typically spend three hours a day in prayer and meditation. I also spend additional time in other forms of prayer including liturgy. As a Pastor I have a reasonable amount of experience in helping people and discipling them in the spiritual life in Christ.

This little book will aim at being simple, yet wise, practical and spiritual. I make no apologies on using an ancient book upon which to write this one. I have learned to come to history from a place of humility and allow it to teach me.

My hope is that this book will open up the doors to start you on to a richer and more experiential prayer life that is full of meaning and joy. I also pray that this book will encourage you to enlarge your own library with wonderful literature from before the Reformation. Trust me you will be blessed in wonderful ways.

One final thought, this little devotional manual is one that cannot be casually read. One must read slowly and carefully to glean the ancient wisdom that is enclosed in this treatise.   This is a book that will need to be read over and over again.

To get a copy of the original 'The Abbey of the Holy Ghost.' I highly recommend a translation into English by Kathryn Anderson Hall, Phd.   It is published through Archway publishing and is available from most good book stores and Amazon.

Kathryn translates the treatise in chapter 5 of her book. Chapters 1-4 looks at the history and influence of this book during the medieval period. The full title to her book is, 'The Abbey of the Holy Ghost, Margaret of York, Charles the Bold, and the politics of Devotion.'

This book will introduce you to various nuns. They will have names such as Lady Wisdom or Dame charity. These nuns are metaphors for Christian virtues which we need to have active in our lives, to enable us to grow in intimacy with God.

May God richly bless you and help you as you embark upon the sacred work of building the abbey of the Holy Ghost within.

Layout of a typical abbey

As you read this book, you may come across terms that are unfamiliar. Please use the map and key to help assist in understanding what an abbey looks like and how it is typically comprised.

1. Church Building. Most abbeys have a church or chapel integral to the layout of an abbey. Within the church building there maybe chapels which are smaller areas with an altar for quiet devotion.

2. The abbey cellar. This is where certain foods and drinks are stored.

3. The kitchen. This is the place where cooking and food preparation takes place.

4. The Refectory. This is a room used for communal meals.

5. The Cloister. This is an area in a monastery around which the principle buildings are arranged. This was also a place where communication between buildings typically took place.

6. The Chapter house. This room is a part of the monastery in which various meetings are held.

7. Sacristy. This is a room where a priest prepares for a service, where vestments and articles of worship are kept.

West Front

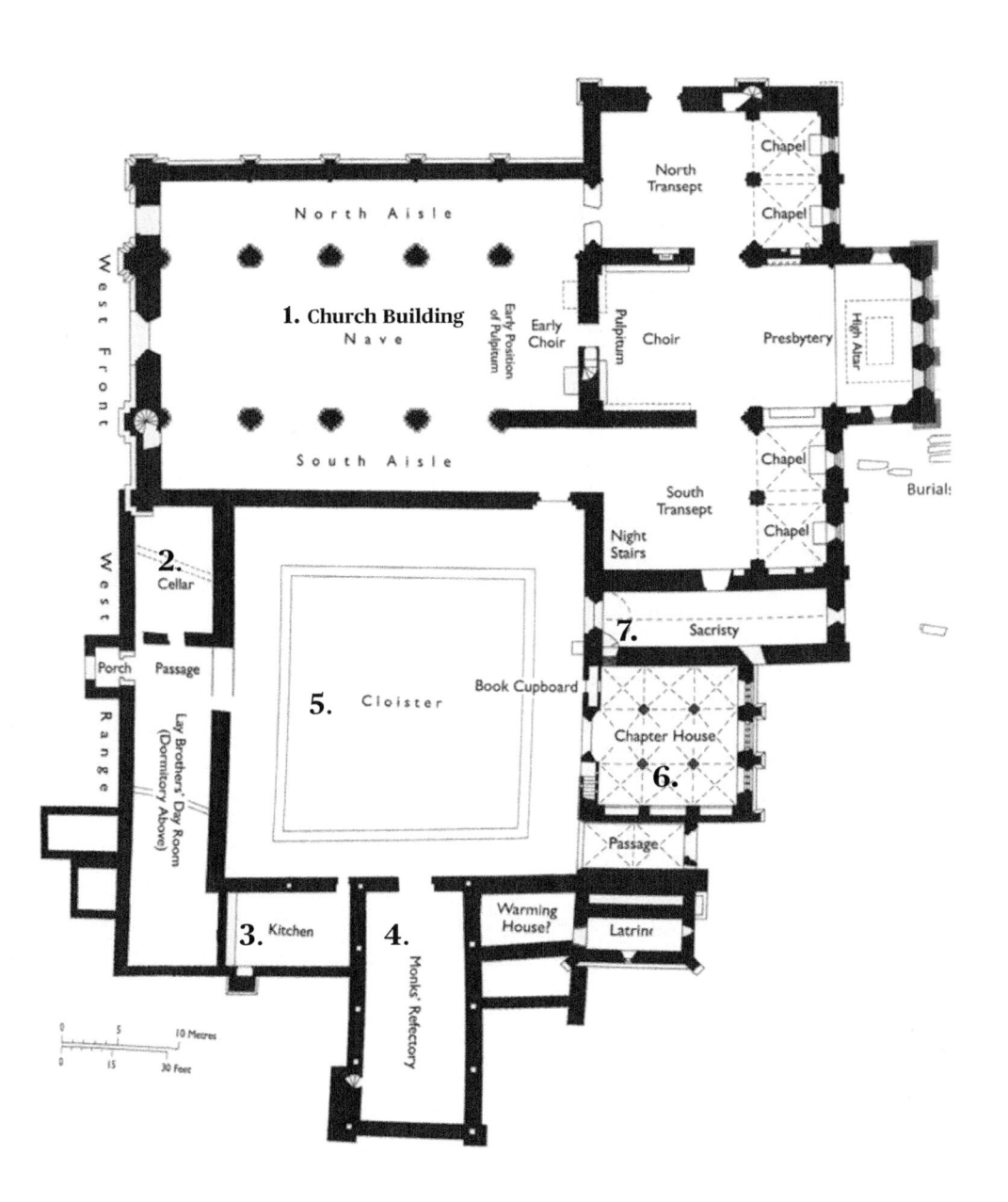

North Aisle

1. Church Building
Nave

South Aisle

Early Position of Pulpitum

Early Choir

Pulpitum

Choir

Presbytery

High Altar

North Transept

Chapel

Chapel

South Transept

Chapel

Chapel

Burials

Night Stairs

2. Cellar

West Range

Porch

Passage

Lay Brothers' Day Room (Dormitory Above)

5. Cloister

Book Cupboard

7. Sacristy

6. Chapter House

Passage

3. Kitchen

4. Monks' Refectory

Warming House?

Latrine

0 5 10 Metres
0 15 30 Feet

1. All may find this abbey in their soul

❖

There are many of us who are feeling the call more and more to earnestly pray. Maybe you have felt the call to join prayer groups or houses of prayer, yet even in this there is still that hunger and yearning for more. Many of us simply cannot afford to go on long retreats, or have much time to even get out of the house. Some may even want to give up their lives and become a monk or nun, but even here you know that this is simply not practically possible.

The Abbey of the Holy Ghost is a place you can build within your life. It is a sacred place in your heart, your own personal monastic space where you can enjoy God and learn the disciplines of the spiritual life.

Our hearts are often places of great darkness and brokenness. The Prophet Jeremiah says, *"The heart is perverse above all things, and unsearchable, who can know it?"*[1]

Yet it is in this place that the Holy Spirit wants to do His wonderful work. In taking us from the darkness of night to the brightness of full day, He wants us to grow in wisdom, understanding and become mature in our Christlike nature.

If we are to have this abbey in our hearts, we need to do a lot of ground work to the gardens of our souls. We need to clear the ground of the thorns and thistles of anger, unforgiveness and evil passions. We need to take the time to make the ground clear, so that we may lay good foundations upon which to build our abbey.

Our hearts are difficult places to understand. With a daily shifting topography, we are at the peril of tempestuous emotions that drive us hard in a direction one day and then a different direction another. How can we come to the place of peace and contentment if we actually have none or very little to begin with?

To gain this peace we need to start clearing the ground, which means we have to tidy up our lives a bit. Maybe there are things going on in our lives, which if we are honest with ourselves, are not conducive to our walk with God. Maybe it's time to stop watching certain TV programs or films. Time to stop reading literature which is not helpful to you as a Christian.

There have been times in my own life where I have had things which I just didn't want to let go off. It was a part of

---

[1] Jeremiah 17:9

my identity and I didn't think it would matter much to God. Yet deep down I knew that it wasn't God's best for me.

One of these unhelpful anchors in my life was my love for an old English prog rock band called Hawkwind. I loved them, I was a complete fan of their music. I had so many of their albums and collectors editions it wasn't funny. It was my obsession and my collection was enviable. I had been collecting their music since my teen years and it was so much a part of my life that I just couldn't or wouldn't get rid of it.

However I felt the Holy Spirit dealing with me on this issue and one day my young son asked me why I listened to music that was not about God. I knew there and then that it had to go. My Hawkwind collection was sold and bought by a collector, who gave me a good price for it. So God was kind to me. I was surprised how my relationship with God leapt forward after this simple step of obedience.

There may be things in our lives that are bad and some things that may seem innocuous. Yet when He calls us to obey Him, we should always obey. God always has our best interest at heart, if we do what He asks it will open to us wonderful new vistas to explore in Him.

Sometimes we need to ask ourselves some hard questions. For example, the Passion of Christ. Is it *The* Passion of Christ, or is it merely *A* Passion of Christ? There is nothing wrong with having interests and hobbies in themselves, for we all need to unwind and do extra curriculum activities. It only becomes an issue when our hobbies and activities become *The* Passion in our lives.

Anything that takes precedence over Christ being lord in our hearts is not healthy business for the soul.

Some may argue that it is surely the work of the Holy Spirit to clean up our hearts? Yes this is true, but we have to work with the Holy Spirit to make those changes. If the Holy Spirit wants to clean up our lives but we are hanging onto things which prevent the Holy Spirit from doing this, then it should be obvious that we have a part to play.

We cannot change our human nature, only God can change that, but we can clean up the mess in our lives to allow the Holy Spirit to do His wonderful work in making us Christ like. If we are to build the Abbey of the Holy Ghost, then we need to make space for the foundations to be laid down.

The bible says, '*Draw nigh to God and He will draw nigh to you. Cleanse your hands, ye sinners: and purify your hearts, ye double minded.*'[2]

When we take the time to make room for God and we are serious, He will take our heart and do wonderful and marvellous things. Our God is a kind and generous God. If we give Him an inch, He will give us a mile. He truly is the God that makes '*My cup runneth over.*'[3] Bless His Holy Name.

---

[2] James 4:8. KJV

[3] Psalm 23:5. KJV

Prayer

Dear Lord Jesus my Holy Saviour.
I bless and praise your wonderful Holy Name.
I Pray that you will send your Holy Spirit.
Make me aware of the things you wish to change.
Give me the strength and courage to accept Your leadings.
Set me on the path of freedom,
And lead me in the paths of righteousness
Amen

2. The Holy Spirit, good walls and the four ladies.

❖

To prepare our abbey to be enclosed with good walls, the Holy Spirit will need to send in some ladies to help get the job done. Their names are Lady Truth, Lady Purity, Lady Humility and Lady Poverty. These ladies are nuns who represent Christian virtues.

Lady Truth and Lady Purity are essential to enable us to guard our hearts from impurity and wicked thoughts. We all have a governess in our hearts that dictates our behaviour. This is why it's really important we learn to love God and His ways. This will then enable us to walk in more truth and purity each day of our lives. Better to have a godly governess that leads to life and peace, than a sinful one that leads to misery and slavery.

So how does one move closer to living in truth and purity? Firstly it is something we should all desire, yearn and pray for each day. We may not even be aware that we should desire such things. Yet God in His mercy will take us where we are at and lead us on the *paths of righteousness for His name's sake.*[4] For He is the Good Shepherd and He wants to lead us into the ways of prayer and contemplation, which leads to the heart of intimacy in our abbey.

Often we wrestle and struggle with bad habits and sinful behaviour in our lives, yet sometimes no matter how hard we try we cannot seem to break free of our sinful ways. Such things can make a soul who is hungry for God weary and sad. We should never give up and yes we will often fail but there is a path which Jesus calls us to, the path of righteousness. It is a narrow path, one which is difficult to walk down but it is also a joyous path.   We can always take comfort even when we fail, for God has a plan for us.

"If we confess our sins, he is faithful and just, to forgive us our sins, and to cleanse us from all iniquity."[5]

It is important to note, the Holy Spirit first sends us Lady Truth and Lady Purity. Although they come hand in hand, it is Lady Truth who we are introduced to first. Indeed one cannot know Lady Purity without first knowing Lady Truth. It is in knowing the truth that one learns a love for that which is pure.   We cannot know what is pure, unless we first encounter the truth of God's word.   The purpose of Lady Truth and Purity, is to protect the heart and soul of the believer from straying into the paths of sin.

---

[4] Psalm 23:3. KJV

[5] 1 John 1:9. Douay Rheims

To know Truth is to know Purity. To know Truth intimately is to be acquainted with her ways which leads us to the path of purity. The way of Truth and Purity is the way of love. Jesus says, *"He who loves Me, will obey Me."*[6]

We need to be very careful to live our lives in love and devotion to Christ. The moment we obey Him from a place of coldness is a moment of great danger for the saint. For here is the worst kind of religion of them all. To obey God without love is an abomination of the worst kind. All that we do must be lived from the place of faith and love. Without faith and love our religion is vain and useless. The Apostle Paul makes this abundantly clear in his letter to the Corinthians. [7]

"If I speak in the tongues of men and of angels, but have not love, I am a noisy gong or a clanging cymbal. And if I have prophetic powers, and understand all mysteries and all knowledge, and if I have all faith, so as to remove mountains but have not love, I am nothing. If I give away all I have, and if I deliver my body to be burned, but have not love, I gain nothing."

To enable Truth to lead us to Purity we must have a love for them both. Indeed one will always lead to another. You will never say, "I love truth but hate purity." For such a statement shows one has not attained to the knowledge of the truth at all.

---

[6] John 14:23

[7] 1 Corinthians 13:1-3 RSV

Lady Purity leads our hearts and minds to dwell on the sweet things of God and the way of faith and love. She is a lady at our side, who constantly reminds us of the scripture which says, *"Finally, brothers and sisters, whatever is true, what ever is noble, whatever is right, whatever is pure, whatever is lovely, whatever is admirable - if anything is excellent or praiseworthy - think about such things."*[8]

Lady Purity is always beckoning and encouraging us to refrain from lustful ways, foul talk, negative thoughts and words. She is always trying to lift us up from the darkness of our nature and raises our chin upwards, so that we may gaze upon Christ and see His glory. "Look not down." She says with kindness in her eyes. "Rather look up to the throne room of heaven and let your meditation and contemplation be on Christ and His wonderfulness. Let the gaze of Him and Him alone be what your heart dwells upon. For you become like that which you behold."

Lady Truth and Lady Purity will protect our hearts from the evil governess of Lady Shame and Bitterness. A heart that rejoices in the truth, is a heart that understands wisdom and the ways of righteousness. It is a heart that understands the fear of the Lord is the foundation stone of life and wisdom. Such a heart will not need to fear shame or the paths of wickedness. The Holy Spirit is always with us, He will never fail or forsake us. Let us therefore allow Lady Truth and Lady Purity to guide our ways.

The next two ladies the Holy Spirit sends is Lady Humility and Lady Poverty. Humility is so key to the

---

[8] Philippians 4:8 NIV

spiritual life in Christ. Without it we do such harm to our precious souls and end up causing much pain to others as well. Lady Humility helps us to dig deep foundations into the hard ground of our hearts. Humility is the place of dying to oneself and being free to serve and become Christ like.

'Then Jesus said to his disciples, "Whoever wishes to come after me must deny himself, take up his cross, and follow me. For whoever wishes to save his life will lose it, but whoever loses his life for my sake will find it."[9]

The path of true spiritual life is when we let go of ourselves and deny ourselves. Jesus warned us to never deny Him, yet He actively encourages us to deny ourselves. Why is this? To understand the life of peace and joy in God, one must realise that as believers in Christ we are already dead. We have no right to ourselves any more as Christians. We once used our bodies as slaves to sin but we now use them in service to God as slaves of righteousness.

'Yet I live, no longer I, but Christ lives in me, insofar as I now live in the flesh, I live by faith in the Son of God who loved me and given himself up for me.[10]

Lady Humility always leads us back to the teachings of Jesus as the mentor and role model for true humility. He is after all our God, King, Lord and Master. In His incarnation He was never arrogant or proud, never pushed His agenda

---

[9] Matthew 16:24-25 NABRE

[10] Galatians 2:20 NABRE

upon people. Rather, He was humble and led by example. For He is the good Shepherd and the sheep who know Him and hear His voice, follow His lead.

'But among you it will be different. Those who are the greatest among you should take the lowest rank, and the leader should be like a servant.'[11]

We must always remember to walk the path of humility, always being gentle, courteous and kind. One should never push themselves to self promotion. For it is in the place of humility that true promotion arises. Never aspire to be anyone, except one who aspires to love Jesus more and more. Let Lady Humility have her way, to help you dig the foundations deep, upon which you can build the strong walls of your spiritual abbey.

How does one serve if one is already a leader in the eyes of man? Simple. If Jesus has placed you into a place of leadership, which is really servanthood, be humble and fulfil your calling with a true heart of simplicity, devotion and love to Him and His people. To resist the call is the way of pride, to embrace the call is true humility. Everyone who obeys the Lord in humility are truly followers of Him.

Lady humility is one who can truly set us free from the vices of our flesh. When one walks the path of humility, one is free to enjoy life, without the human heart wanting to be seen as one who has importance in the eyes of man. When you know that your worth is found in Christ alone,

---

[11] Luke 22:26. NLT

you can attain a joy and freedom more precious than money could ever hope to purchase.

The final lady sent to help us is known as Lady Poverty. Why would the Holy Spirit send such a woman to help us build our abbey? One may ask, "How can poverty be in any way helpful?" However, a little thought and reflection will help us see the wisdom of poverty and why she is needed in our abbey.

Did not Jesus say to us, *"Blessed are the poor in spirit, for theirs is the kingdom of heaven."*[12] To have a poor spirit is key to having a co-share in the kingdom of heaven. If you want to become rich in God, you must first become poor and poverty stricken of yourself. Don't ever come to God thinking you have something to offer Him which He can use. One may think this thinking may be seen as commendable, it is actually anything but.

We first need to realise that God needs nothing from anyone. We need to understand that we need everything from God. Without Him we have no life, no breath, no existence, nothing. He is the source of all life and all that we are and have is from Him and belongs to Him alone. Our gifting, our skillsets, our personalities all ultimately come from God.

True enlightenment comes when we realise that without God we are truly nothing. All that we have and are comes from Him.

---

[12] Matthew 5:3 NABRE

Lady Poverty must first help us to understand that although we have gifts and talents, they all come from God and must therefore be rendered and submitted to Him and His will. There is no room for pride and self importance with Lady Poverty, she will simply not stand for such behaviour or thinking. Why is she like this? Because the work of this lady is to help us attain a joy and freedom that glorification of self could never give.

When we realise that all we are is from God and not from ourselves, our reality and mindset shifts from our abilities to God's. Our abilities is changed from ourselves to Jesus and His Holy Spirit, who empowers us to live day by day.

'Finally, draw your strength from the Lord and from His mighty power.'[13]

When we learn the discipline of living our lives from God and not ourselves, we realise that in truth we are poor in spirit. Yet knowing and understanding our poverty of spirit is the key to being rich in spirit. The Holy Spirit *'will fully supply whatever you need, in accord with His glorious riches in Christ Jesus.'*[14]

The world around may laugh at Lady Poverty, thinking her to be worthless but to the saint she is truly beautiful to behold. She teaches the way to riches in the Spirit of God, that no other can show.

---

[13] Ephesians 6:10. NABRE

[14] Philippians 4:19. NABRE

We must thank God everyday for these four virtues, without them and their teachings, we would simply fail in building our spiritual abbey. Without that abbey of the soul, we will never attain to the place of spiritual intimacy with God that we all so dearly desire.

Prayer

O Jesus my sweet desire,
How my heart longs for thee,
Send me Truth, Purity, Humility and Poverty.
That Thee I may know and truly see.

Amen

3. Obedience, Mercy, Patience and Strength.

❖

A well designed and thought out abbey must be near a source of water. For water is the source of life and cleansing. There are streams of waters our abbey requires, the water of the word of God, the water from the Holy Spirit of God, and the salty water of our tears.

The sacred scriptures washes us and keeps us clean in the knowledge and ways of the living God. The scriptures are essential for the church and indeed for our abbey. *'To sanctify her (the church), cleansing her by the bath of water with the word. That He might present to Himself the church in splendour, without spot or wrinkle or any such thing, that she might be holy and without blemish.'* [15]

Our bucket to draw from the streams must be the daily practise of meditation on the word of God. To meditate upon scripture is the only way to plummet the refreshing depths and benefits of the water of delights. Meditation upon sacred scripture opens us to a world of intimacy with the Spirit of God in ways very little else can.

'Blessed is the man who does not walk in the counsel of the wicked, nor stands in the way of sinners, nor sit in company with scoffers. Rather, the law of the LORD is his joy; and on his law he meditates day and night. He is like a tree planted near streams of water, that yields its fruit in season; its leaves never wither; whatever he does prospers.' [16]

In addition to meditating on the scriptures, praying the scriptures, reading, studying and even singing the scriptures, we also need to drink from the sweet and loving Holy Spirit. The scriptures encourage us to have communion and fellowship with Him all the time.

'The grace of the Lord Jesus Christ and the love of God and the fellowship of the Holy Spirit be with you all.' [17]

---

[15] Ephesians 5:26-27 NABRE

[16] Psalm 1 NABRE

[17] 2 Corinthians 13:13 NABRE

We must practise the continual presence and awareness of God at all times and in all situations and in all circumstances.

'My presence will go with you, and I will give you rest.' [18]

'You will show me the path to life, abounding joy in your presence, the delights at your right hand forever.' [19]

One strategy to employ to keep aware of God and His presence is to pray at the cardinal hours of the day. In addition to your prayer time with God, endeavour to pray at 9am, 12pm, 3pm and 6pm. This is known as praying the hours. At these times read a couple of psalms and some written prayers from prayer books and church liturgy.

One may ask, "how is this possibly a spiritual exercise?" Surely something spiritual is less formulaic and free? Actually no. Indeed praying the hours is a tradition the church and the Jewish people have kept for thousands of years. The most beneficial spiritual growth comes through basic discipline, this is how we grow and mature.

'At dusk, dawn and noon I will grieve and complain, and my prayer will be heard.' [20]

---

[18] Exodus 33:14. ESV

[19] Psalm 16:11 NABRE

[20] Psalm 55:17 (18) NABRE

'...And he (Daniel) continued kneeling on his knees three times a day, praying and giving thanks before his God, as he had been doing previously.' [21]

Praying the hours and using set prayers and liturgy has always been a beautiful way of enriching one's walk with God. Because of the use of liturgy, our own personal prayers will become more expressive in language and enable us to communicate better how we feel.

Praying at the cardinal hours of the day, helps to reset one's focus from the world back to God. It centres us and enables the soul to focus on the things of God and not the world. Praying the hours enables one to become more reflective on the living and active presence of God in our lives each day. This simple spiritual discipline will add a whole other dimension to our spiritual walk with God. This way of life will also be of great benefit to the building up of our spiritual abbey.

Our abbey must be founded not just upon the waters of the word and the Holy Spirit but also upon the tears of repentance.

To better understand the things of holiness and God, one also needs to understand how sinful we really are. Without God and His grace we cannot stand or enter into His presence. Coming to God with the daily offering of repentance and seeking forgiveness is essential to our spiritual nurturing. We must understand that every careless sin cost Jesus dearly in agony upon the cross.

---

[21] Daniel 6:10 NASB

It is important that we never become casual or indifferent to sin no matter how seemingly small they maybe in our eyes. To truly understand the fear of God and His holiness we must become aware of our nature and constant reliance upon God's grace to forgive and sustain us.

The waters of repentance, the word of God and the Holy Spirit will bring great joy and sustenance to our spiritual Abbey of the Holy Ghost.

'The stream of the river maketh the city of God joyful: the most High hath sanctified his own tabernacle.' [22]

It is this river of waters that keeps the city of our soul and conscience clean, pure and abundant in fruitfulness. For we live within a city within a city. We are of a kingdom that cannot be shaken. We walk as pilgrims on this earth whilst in our hearts we carry the realm of heaven which shines forth from us. We carry the bread of life in our souls and become sacred tabernacles of the presence of God to all around us.

We now come to two primary ladies who will help us in our Abbey, Lady Obedience and Lady Mercy. These ladies walk with us side by side and enable much joyous fruit to grow in our Abbey garden.

These two ladies represent obedience and mercy, righteousness and love. Our Lord says it well when He

---

[22] Psalm 45:5 Douay-Rheims

says, *'if you love me, you will obey me.'* [23] The apostle John also reiterates those sacred words, *'And by this we know that we have known him, if we keep His commandments.'* [24]

Love and obedience go together like a pair of beautiful gloves. One for each hand and together they make a perfect pair, a match made in heaven. Indeed love and obedience is a sweet honey from heaven itself.

These two ladies are essential to helping us build the walls of our faith and our religion great and high. We show obedience for God by loving all and being generous to the poor. As we have freely received God's grace, love, compassion and generosity, so we too must share those things to others.

Jesus gave us a new and great commandment which we must daily observe in prayer, word and deed. *'A new commandment I give you: Love one another as I have loved you. So you must love one another.'*[25]

It is because of our great love for God that we are motivated to do good works for others. Indeed the outworking of our salvation is through faith and good works.

---

[23] John 14:15

[24] 1 John 2:3 Douay Rheims

[25] John 13:34 NIV

'You see that a person is justified by works and not faith alone.'[26]

To say we have faith and then ignore the plight of the needy is no faith at all. Knowing that we are loved by God inspires us to love Him and those around us. By doing good works according to the Great Commandment of Jesus and by the counsel of our Holy Mother - The Church, we end up building our abbey walls strong and high with wonderful stones of good works.

The cement that binds our stones together in the wall is faith. Without faith in God, motivated by His Spirit and love is sadly a dead work. Our rewards in God come from the place of living faith and love toward God. Faith, hope and love are the greatest of all virtues, yet the greatest of those three is love. Love of God, love for God, true love of true love. For our God is a God of love and we are His dearly beloved children. Let us therefore be imitators of Him, our Beloved King of Majesty and Love.

Because all our works must be motivated by our love for God we must therefore be compassionate to the unbeliever in our prayers. For their works of kindness and charity is as filthy rags to God. Good deeds will never obtain the mercy of salvation. Only those who believe by faith and works will obtain Christ's free merit of salvation.

The next two ladies to help us in the construction of our Abbey is Lady Patience and Lady Strength. They are two great pillars which sustain and hold aloft the works of the

---

[26] James 2:24. NASB

saint in the building of the Abbey of the soul. Patience and Strength are two important virtues for the believer to walk in. For with them, one can be consistent and true, even through the most arid and arduous of times. Many temptations and tribulations may buffet us like a strong wind against the shore. However, providing we stand true in faith, prayer and love, we will remain strong and resilient with the help of Lady Patience and her sister Lady Strength.

'Finally, brethren, be strengthened in the Lord, and in the might of his power.' [27]

'Rejoice in hope, be patient in suffering, persevere in prayer.[28]

'And thus Abraham, having patiently endured, obtained the promise.'[29]

---

[27] Ephesians 6:10. Douay Rheims

[28] Romans 12:12. NRSV

[29] Hebrews 6:15. NRSV

Prayer

Oh my dear sweet Jesus.
Please help me in my weakness to love your sacred scriptures
more and more.
Teach me to meditate upon your decrees and laws,
that I may live a life holy and pleasing to you.
Teach me to confess my sins often,
For I long to be a clean house for you to dwell in.
Let me be a vessel of your love,
Let me shine to all around.
Help me to become strong and true,
So that my life may glorify You.
Amen.

4. The house founded upon seven pillars, that Lady Wisdom built.

❖

The book of Proverbs teaches us that Lady Wisdom built a house that was beautiful and grand to behold.[30] The foundations of that house was built upon the seven pillars of wisdom itself. This is in stark contrast to the Lady of Worldly Wisdom who is also known as the harlot. She built her house and founded it upon the stairway which leads to death and hades.[31]

In building our spiritual abbey we must not build using worldly wisdom, for that would be folly of the greatest undertaking. Indeed the world with all its vain ideologies and philosophies is opposed to the ways of God and His

---

[30] Proverbs 9:1

[31] Proverbs 5:5

teachings. We do not build our faith upon worldliness and wisdom which is earthy and demonic.[32] Rather we build our lives upon the sacred wisdom of God Himself. This is a wisdom that is beautiful and divine and comes from heaven above. [33]

What are the seven pillars which Lady Wisdom built her house upon? They are faith, hope, love, justice, temperance, fortitude and prudence.

Upon these seven pillars, our abbey is sustained and maintained. For the Holy Spirit lives in these beautiful virtues and we move and have our being in Him.[34] It is our duty and privilege to disciple ourselves to live in and upon these seven pillars.

If we build our abbey upon these foundations we will surely build great and true. These foundations will enable us to weather the worst of storms and floods which the enemy and this fallen world throw at us.

We are all bearers of the kingdom of God, it is alive in us through the blessed Holy Spirit, who has come and made His home in our hearts. To live in the power of the kingdom of God, one must learn to live by its decrees, ordinances and customs. We are thus residents of another realm and we live by the ways of that realm.

---

[32] James 3:15

[33] James 3:17-18

[34] Acts 17:28

We are in this world of darkness, but we are merely pilgrims and ambassadors passing through. In the world today every country has an embassy to represent the government of another. Our abbey of the Holy Ghost is a holy and sacred place, an embassy of the Kingdom of heaven, where the rule of God and His ways are practised and lived.

To truly experience more of the divine, we must build with materials of the divine. We cannot and must never build our abbey on the ways of this world, but upon the seven pillars of God and His wisdom.

Our abbey represents heaven and a place for God to dwell in by His sacred presence. Therefore this house of God must be made from sacred and holy materials. Never use materials from the house of the harlot, that is to say, worldly wisdom. Rather let us build true and strong upon the seven pillars of the house which Lady Wisdom herself built upon.

Prayer

Dear Lord Jesus,

My sweet and precious Saviour.

Let me this day build my life upon the rock of your wisdom and teachings.

May I live according to the ways of faith, hope, love, justice, temperance, fortitude and prudence.

Teach me Jesus by Your sacred and precious Holy Spirit,

To live my life daily upon those seven pillars.

Help me to be a clean vessel and temple for you to dwell in.

Let my life be a pleasant and sweet aroma.

In Your sacred Name I ask.

Amen.

5. The cloister of the abbey and the structure of the abbey's offices.

❖

The cloister is the central part of the abbey which the principle buildings are arranged round about. It is normally square in structure, an open quadrangle, with the church, refectory, chapter house and apartment buildings on each side. The cloister is the heart of the abbey which links all the other buildings together. The cloister gets its name from the simple fact that it is enclosed and guarded on all four corners.

If we are to be truly pious, we must understand that we need to have hearts and minds that are closed to everything but Jesus and that which is pure and noble. We need to be chaste in heart, mind and deed if we are to walk the religious life in God. Every abbey has gates and doors and we must be mindful what we open and when. Our eye, ear and mouth gates can bring great joy or deep regret to our sensitive soul. Averting the eyes, closing our ears and keeping our mouths from slander and gossip are essential to walking the life of piety.

The ancient church fathers encouraged Christians not to laugh too much. For in much jesting and mirth there tends to be talk that is not always clean and right before the Lord. Our speech can grieve the Spirit of God and thus defile our souls. We must therefore endeavour to master our tongues and emotions when it comes to the religious life. Remember, one of the fruits of the Spirit is self control.[35]

Ephesians 4:29-30. *'No foul language should come out of your mouths, but only such as is good for needed edification, that it may impart grace to those who hear. And do not grieve the Holy Spirit of God, with which you were sealed for the day of redemption.'* NABRE

Matthew 15:11. *'It is not what enters one's mouth that defiles a person; but what comes out of the mouth is what defiles one.'* NABRE

The four walls of our cloister are the eyes, the ears, the mouth and the heart. We must learn to diligently guard these, especially the heart. For out of the heart flow the very issues of life itself.[36] Our heart is a very special and sensitive place for the spiritual life. However, it is

---

[35] Galatians 5:23

[36] Proverbs 4:23

important that we understand that there is a difference between the mind and the heart.

The mind is constantly assessing and judging and rarely lives in the moment. It is always thinking about what has been, what could have been and what could be. Yet God is only ever experienced in the now, not yesterday or tomorrow. It is the heart that can truly live in the moment with God. Only the heart can contemplate and meditate upon God.

We need our mind for everyday activities, but when it comes to the things of God and the Spirit. The mind often gets distracted and gets in the way of our spiritual progress in God. It loves to constantly think about anything else but that which it should think and dwell on when it comes to God. We need our intellect to help us understand our bibles and doctrine but in the area of prayer our mind needs to be placed in neutral as the soul starts to take charge.

The soul is capable of living in the moment and experiencing God in ways the mind cannot. Our soul is our heart. This is why we must guard and protect it with all due diligence. We must learn to close our heart from all wicked and lustful thinking. We need to take every thought captive as the sacred scriptures command us to do.[37]

We need to be well guarded by the four walls of our cloister. We need to lower our eyes and our gaze from anything that would bring angst and disruption to our

---

[37] 2 Corinthians 10:5

hearts. Close our ears to all that pertains to evil, gossip and slander. Close our mouths to all evil and corrupt speech, speaking evil of no man.[38]

Whoever guards himself in respect to the four aspects of eyes, ears, mouth and heart does well and is certainly on the path of piety.

Lady Confession is the chapter house of our little abbey. One cannot underestimate the importance and power of confession in the religious life. Sin creates a barrier between man and God[39] and thus we would do well to keep a short account and walk in His eternal kindness, mercy and forgiveness. If we confess our sins, then our dear heavenly Father will forgive us our sins, through the precious blood of Christ.[40]

Lady Prudence shall be the refectory. In our abbey one must have prudence to govern and discipline oneself by the use of the teachings of Christ. Prudence is considered to be one of the four Cardinal virtues that we should strive to attain. Without prudence, that is self discipline, our religious life will simply never grow or amount to anything that will bring lasting joy, change and eternal reward.

Lady Orison (Worship), the lady of prayer shall be the chapel. It surely needs not be said of the importance of

---

[38] Titus 3:2

[39] Isaiah 59:2

[40] 1 John 1:9

prayer in the religious life. Indeed prayer is our very oxygen of life and relationship with God. We pray to God through liturgy, psalms, prayers from the heart, praying in the Spirit, praying supplications and intercessions. Lady Orison is the chapel of our abbey. The chapel must be a place which is visited frequently every day.

Lady Contemplation is the dormitory. This dormitory must be up high and raised off the ground. Contemplation is essential to engage in a wonderful appreciation of Christ, His nature, His ways and His creation. Contemplation is a must in helping us to see the deeply spiritual world we live in. It is a discipline that will help to raise us up over our base carnal nature and desires. This is why the dormitory must be up high. Its elevation denotes its importance in the life of the pious.

To be truly contemplative one must learn to close the door to strife, fear and worry. Such emotions have no place in the life of the contemplative. These emotions will take away our peace and rob us of contemplating God's divine goodness that is all around us. To be contemplative is to have eyes to see, ears to hear and a heart that perceives spiritual truth that is in the scriptures and in the world around us. The natural world of creation in all its beauty is constantly telling us of the glory of God and His invisible attributes. It takes a contemplative heart to hear and see what creation is revealing and telling us.[41]

Lady Compassion shall be the infirmary. Compassion is a very important virtue to attain. Our good Lord and Saviour

---

[41] Psalm 19:1-6. Also see Romans 1:20

Jesus taught us the way of kindness and compassion. We cannot live the religious life and be mean and hard hearted. We must never be critical and judgemental, rather we should be kind and compassionate to those around us. We all struggle in many areas of life and we appreciate God being compassionate toward our weaknesses. Therefore as we have freely received from God, so must also we freely give to others that which God has so lavishly laboured upon us.

Lady Devotion is the cellarer in our abbey, thus love must underpin everything in our lives. One of the great hallmarks of the pious is devotion to our Lord and Master, Jesus Christ. Devotion to God is not a legalistic, cold, rigoristic devotion, rather it is something that is born aloft upon the wings of love. Everything we do for our Lord must be motivated by love for Him. Jesus said that if we love Him we will obey Him.[42] Obedience and devotion must be fuelled by love and love alone. For the greatest of all the virtues is love as taught in First Corinthians, Chapter Thirteen. Love is the greatest of all virtues for it is the very nature of God Himself.

1 John 4:16 *'So we have known and believe the love that God has for us.* **_God is love_**, *and those who abide in love abide in God and God abides in them.'* NRSV. (Emphasis added)

Finally and by no means least, is Lady Meditation. She shall be the granary of our Abbey of the Holy Ghost. The granary is the place where all the grain is stored and from this grain much food is made. Meditation or mental prayer

---

[42] John 14:15

as it is sometimes known, is so important to the religious life that its benefit and prominence cannot be stressed enough. Meditation is the key to growing in the knowledge of God. This is not merely a head knowledge, rather it is an intimate knowledge that reveals the heartbeat of God. Meditation brings intimacy with the living God in a way few other spiritual disciplines can.   Meditation upon the scriptures is the gateway into this wonderful intimacy with God. This form of practice is often known as *'Lectio Divina.'*

Finally dear reader it needs to be noted that Lady Compassion, Devotion and Meditation must be in abundance within the abbey. For without such, life in the abbey would simply be unsustainable.

Let's conclude this chapter with a short prayer.

Prayer

Oh my dear sweet Lord and Saviour Jesus.
I pray and thank you today for Your teachings and Your ways.
Help me to understand the ways of Your Spirit and help me to understand the words of this book.
Teach me, show me, reveal to my eyes the wonders of Your ways.
Let my heart perceive and understand that which you want me to know and understand of you.
Lord by Your Holy Spirit and Your good grace please help me to daily build you abbey in my heart.

Amen.

6. Construct the convent and let God the Father, Son and Holy Ghost build it.

❖

We need to understand that the blessed Holy Spirit is the honoured guard and defender of our religion in Christ. It is He, via the will of the Father and the Son, that endows the sweet dewfall of blessings, virtues and graces daily upon our lives.

The religious life is not merely about instituting daily disciplines such as prayer, fasting, meditation, contemplation and study of scripture; rather, the life of the pious is one that is bathed in God's ways, His love and His power.

The scriptures are clear that we have to live in the strength and power of His might, not our own. [43] We learn to live in His righteousness by daily submitting our life and will more and more to that of the Holy Spirit .[44]

The words of an ancient hymn, '*Nunc, Sancte, nobis, Spiritus,*' teaches and instructs us of a right heart to have and where the source of our religious life comes from:-

Come, Holy Spirit, ever one
With God the Father and the Son,
Send forth your overflowing grace
And with your love our souls embrace.

With all our strength and mind and voice,
We sing your praises and rejoice!
Inflame our hearts with love anew,
May all the world have love for you!

To God the Father and the Son,
To Holy Spirit, three in one.
May praise and honour, glory be
To you, eternal Trinity. Amen.

It is by the sanctifying power and enabling of the Holy Spirit that our covent is established within our abbey. The convent is a community of persons devoted to the religious life, under a superior. For example, there are congregations of nuns, monks or friars and these

---

[43] Ephesians 6:10

[44] 2 Corinthians 5:21 & Romans 12:1-2

congregations are known as societies. Thus within our hearts and our abbey, we need to have a society of virtues and graces under the superior of our blessed Holy Triune God.

It is God alone who establishes the convent in our abbey. We have to daily follow rhythms and disciplines to work with Him to permanently establish by habit that which He alone establishes in our souls. Through daily discipline we slowly but surely construct the abbey, brick by brick, foundation stone by foundation stone. However it is God who truly builds it and forms it into its glorious structure. The scriptures remind us, *'Unless the lord build the house, they labour in vain that build it. Unless the Lord keep the city, he watcheth in vain that keep it.'*[45]

In conclusion to this chapter we need to understand the workings of the Triune God in the work of salvation, sanctification and application in the day to day life of our abbey.

It is God the Father who wants this abbey to be constructed as a place to honour Him, His Son and His blessed Holy Spirit.

'Shall not Zion say: This man and that man is born in her? And the Highest Himself hath founded her.'[46]

---

[45] Psalm 127:1 Douay-Rheims Bible

[46] Psalm 86:5 Douay-Rheims Bible

God the Son by his magnificent wisdom insists and orders the construction of this beautiful abbey.

'Let every soul be subject to higher powers: for there is no power but from God: and those that are, are ordained by God.' [47]

The Holy Spirit is the divine Guardian, Defender and Visitor of this sacred abbey of the heart. Because of this our heart rejoices and sings out the words of this famous ancient hymn, *'Veni Creator Spiritus.'*

Come, Holy Ghost, Creator.
Come from thy bright and heavenly throne;
Come, take possession of our souls,
And make them all thine own.

Thou who art called the Paraclete,
Best gift of God above,
The living spring, the living fire,
Sweet unction and true love.

Thou who art sevenfold in thy grace
Finger of God's right hand;
His promise, teaching little ones to speak
And understand.

O guide our minds with thy blest light,
With love our hearts inflame;
And with thy strength which ne'er decays,
Confirm our mortal frame.

---

[47] Romans 13:1 Douay-Rheims Bible

Far from us drive our deadly foe;
True peace unto us bring;
And through all perils lead us safe,
Beneath thy sacred wing.

Through thee may we the Father know,
Through thee the eternal Son,
And thee the Spirit of them both,
Thrice blessed three in One.

Prayer

Oh my blessed Love, the wondrous Triune God.
Help me to know and understand thee.
Help me have eyes to see, ears to hear and a heart that perceives.
Teach me to be a true disciple of you Jesus, as you were a true disciple of Your Blessed Father.
Let the work of your Holy Ghost by the will of the Father, be ever done each day in my frail heart.
May my life be one that lives to glorify thee,
Oh great, beautiful, sanctifying, merciful God.
Amen.

7. Dame Charity must be abbess of our abbey of the Holy Ghost.

❖

Our abbey has now been built, yet before the convent has sung and called upon the Holy Spirit, we need to put in place a good abbess. The one whom we shall choose, is known as Dame Charity. What a wonderful woman she is, for she is deemed beautiful and wise.

Dame Charity is not a woman whom we are very familiar with in today's Christianity. Charity is not about merely giving alms to the poor, rather charity is a sacrificial, giving love. She is not self seeking or self serving, she is not moved by passions or emotions. Rather Dame Charity is a lady who sacrificially gives of her time, effort, kindness, love, provision and mercy irrespective of how she feels.

As Christ loved us, so must we love all. We cannot pick and choose whom to show this love to. For freely we have received from God and thus freely we must show kindness and mercy to all around.[48]

In the tradition of all abbeys, the abbess or abbott must be adhered to with strict obedience. We must obey our abbess or abbott as though they were Christ Himself. What ever charge they give, we must obey. We cannot do anything, go anywhere, take or give consent without the permission of the abbess. The novitiate simply has no choice in this matter. We must become slaves of Dame Charity.

Our sacred, holy religion and this holy abbey must be protected and established through obedience to our abbess. We must do nothing, go nowhere, take nothing, without the permission of our holy abbess, Dame Charity.

This wonderful walk of pious religion, intimacy with Christ and glorious faith in Him must only ever be done in love, in charity. The Apostle Paul teaches us, *'Let all your things be done in charity.'*[49]

The secret to maintaining our walk with God, in our hearts and thus keeping our abbey in good standing, must come from Dame Charity. Without her and the counsel she brings, we would simply not be able to keep our hearts chaste for Jesus. Our abbey would thus become overgrown

---

[48] Matthew 10:8

[49] 1 Corinthians 16:14. Douay Rheims Version

and choked with weeds and all manner of wild plants and animals.

We walk by Dame Charity's instruction everyday. By doing so it enables us to daily visit our abbey and keep it in order and well maintained. We need to understand that sadly there are many who walk by their own whims and desires against the instructions of the abbess. Christians who refuse to walk according to the ways and disciplines of scripture, pertaining to love, will sadly put themselves into a world of trouble and heartache.

We must walk the walk of love, we must obey the requests of Dame Charity. All our actions, deeds, words and thoughts must be motivated by Dame Charity. *'Let all your things be done in charity.'*

Alas, there are some in religion who do many things, they give and they take, all against the instruction, teachings and commandments of Dame Charity. However if we walk in her often strict ways and commandments, we will show forth the love of God to all around us. Then we can rest assure that our abbey will be beautiful and thus well maintained.

Prayer

Oh sweet Jesus, my Lord and my Love.
Teach me to walk in the ways of Your wonderous love and kindness each day.
Blessed be your sweet and Holy Name.
Amen.

8. Madame Wisdom must be the prioress and Lady Humility the sub prioress of the abbey of the Holy Ghost.

❖

'*Happy are those who find wisdom, and those who get understanding, for her income is better than silver, and her revenue better than gold. She is more precious than jewels, and nothing you desire can compare with her. Long life is in her right hand; in her left hand are riches and honour. Her ways are the ways of pleasantness, and all her paths are peace. She is a tree of life to all who lay hold of her; those who hold her fast are called happy.*'[50]

---

[50] Proverbs 3:13-18. NRSV

The three great ladies in our abbey are Dame Charity who is our abbess, Lady Wisdom who is our prioress and Lady Humility the sub prioress.

Lady Wisdom is rightly our prioress for she is a great, beautiful and wondrous thing to the life of the religious person. God loves wisdom, He created Wisdom and used her to create all things.

'The Lord created me at the beginning of His work, the first of his acts of long ago.' [51]

'The LORD by wisdom founded the earth; by understanding he established the heavens.'[52]

Wisdom is known as 'Sophia,' in the Greek version of the scriptures. She is loved by God and is a special gift to those who fear Him. She is to be highly prized, highly esteemed and highly desired above all treasures. It is for this reason why she must be elevated to be Prioress, in our abbey of the Holy Ghost.

If God, created wisdom and by her created all things, then surely we too need to build our lives on her ways and her teachings? We must adhere to the counsel of our Prioress, in all matters, for her great wisdom will guide us and disciple us to greater depths in our love and knowledge of God, in the spiritual life.

---

[51] Proverbs 8:22. NRSV

[52] Proberbs 3:19 NRSV

If we wish the Great Visitor, the Holy Ghost, to frequent our abbey, we must love our Prioress, 'Sophia,' as He loves her. We must build our lives and our ways on her teachings, just as God laid out the foundations of the earth by her help.

'When He assigned to the sea its limit, so that the waters might not transgress his command, when he marked out the foundations of the earth, then I (wisdom) was beside him, like a master worker; and I was daily his delight.[53]

Oh dear reader, we must understand that Lady Charity and Lady Wisdom are the great ladies of whom we must give our obedience to. The blessed Holy Ghost will smile and rejoice and frequent our abbey often, if we live to serve our abbess and prioress. Obedience to them is quintessential to deepening our relationship with God and allowing our abbey to become a beautiful sanctuary for the blessed Spirit of God.

All our deeds must be done at the behest and counsel of our abbess and prioress. Only the truest and most pure of good deeds and works can be achieved through them. This will rejoice the heart of our blessed Visitor, the Holy Spirit.

The next lady we need to obey and pay great attention to is Lady Humility. She is not interested in being first, rather she seeks to be last and unseen. This is why she is the sub prioress. Yet the blessed Holy Ghost loves her so much and

---

[53] Proverbs 8:29-30. NRSV Parenthesis added.

we would do well to love her as He does. Great joy and peace is found in the place of humility. It is a place of freedom, a place free from the pangs and desires of the flesh to be important or recognised.   In the walk of humility one is enabled to live life with greater stillness of the soul. The world sees Lady Humility as foolish and weak, but to the truly religious soul, they see her for what she really is, blessed holy joy and freedom.

Oh blessed pilgrim, know that this is a good religion and your abbey is a holy abbey, where dwell such wonderful and incredible people. Learn from the ladies whom The blessed Visitor chooses to give to you. Only from obedience to their counsel and instruction will you truly make your abbey worthy of the Sacred One.

These ladies are so saintly, precious and beautiful that we would do well, yes, very well, to imitate them. Praise the Lord and Saviour Jesus, every day for abbess Charity, Prioress Wisdom and sub-prioress Humility.

The blessed, Triune God of Father, Son and Holy Ghost rejoice in these three women. Walk in their footsteps, rejoice in their ways, always be thankful for them. To the world, these women are but nonsensical fools. To the religious they are spiritual masters who lead us on the paths of righteousness, peace and joy, for His Name's sake. Do not hesitate to follow their instruction, for all who follow their ways get to drink deep of God's river of delights.

Do remember reader, that our Lord and Saviour warned us that many will despise us. If the people despised Jesus who walked in the ways of Charity, Wisdom and Humility then expect to be equally despised.

'And you shall be hated of all men for my name's sake: but he that endureth to the end shall be saved. The disciple is not above his master, nor the servant above his lord. It is enough for the disciple that he be as his master, and the servant as his lord. If they called the master of the house Beelzebub, how much more shall they call them of his household.' [54]

Before the days of Christ taking on human flesh the world was in great misery. Our God in His kindness and mercy, lowered the heavens and descended in human form, conceived by the Holy Spirit and became born of the blessed virgin. He came and tabernacled amongst us to teach us the ways of eternal life, the ways of the kingdom of His most holy Father.

Through Jesus and Him alone, can we truly have peace in our souls. God is calling us to the religious life, to follow Him more closely. Jesus said, in John chapter seventeen and verse three, "Eternal life is knowing the Father."

For us to truly know God, we must walk in the way which our beautiful Master and Saviour taught us. Thus let us have hearts that are gentle and humble. Let us allow Charity, Wisdom and Humility to guide us every moment of the day. Having hearts such as these will create a beautiful abbey which the Blessed Holy Spirit, will dwell, reside and shine from.

---

[54] Matthew 10:22 & 24-25. KJV

Prayer

Oh my sweet beautiful Jesus,
Please hear my prayers this day.
Teach me Lord to walk in Your ways,
Help me to walk in Your charity, wisdom and humility.
Let my life become the beautiful fragrance of Jesus.
Let my heart be the abbey which the Holy Spirit, would joyfully reside.
I ask this of Thee in Thy precious, sacred and Holy Name.
Amen.

9. Jesus Christ demonstrated in many ways His great love for us by His incarnation, His passion and His cruel death.

❖

"**M**y dear child, I your Messiah, Jesus, have something that I wish to tell you and want you to take notice of. My life, from its beginning, the middle to the end, was one of poverty, tribulation, agony, hardship and difficulty.

You need to understand that as I was in the flesh, a body, so you, My body, the church, are on this earth. As I suffered in the flesh, so you must also as my body, the church, learn from the mysteries of my suffering.

Look into the gospels and see how I was born. I was born to a poor family and born into poverty. I was not born in comfort and riches in the palaces of kings. I was born in obscurity. I had a meek and lowly entrance to this earth. I was not born into a world where the nations worshiped me, rather I was born in a stable, with animals round about.

Look at how the world hated me even as a child Herod tried to have me killed and commanded the death of the innocents, the first martyrs. He thought he had finally gotten rid of me through this murderous act. Look at how my mother and Joseph transported me to the land of Egypt to hide me from murderous, wicked kings who hated me and the kingdom I represented.

Look at how I managed to live sweetly in the world with you. It was not just for a few days but thirty three years I lived and dwelt amongst you. Look at how I lived as a man look at how I spent my ministry, in teaching the world about the kingdom of My Father and eternal life. I performed signs and wonders and did many marvellous works, to reveal to wicked men the goodness and love of My Father.

Look at how the world was never satiated with being evil toward me and how I was never satiated in being loving and kind in return. Look how I turned the wickedness of evil toward Me and converted it to good.

Yet for all the kindness and love I showed this world, it still felt inclined to grab me, slap me, arrest me, betray me, spit on me and blaspheme against me. Then after all this, it chose to whip my flesh with cruel whips, tearing my flesh to pieces. It condemned me to die the death of criminals and drove metal spikes into my flesh, as it nailed me to a cross to be crucified.

Listen to me my dear child, I bore these terrible hardships, I chose to bear them. No human could have ever taken my life, unless My Father and I had willed it. But we did will it to be so. I allowed man to be cruel to me, so that I could show you how much I love you and thus pay the heavy penalty for your freedom. The love that I have for you is beyond your natural understanding, beyond human reasoning. As every insult, slap, betrayal, wicked whip and nail struck me, I endured the pain through love. I looked forward in love, to the day in time when you would eventually turn and love me in return.

My love for you is so strong, so real and so powerful. Everything I endured, I endured for you, because of my great love for you. My dear child, my hunger and thirst is for you and your eternal well being. It was love, not cords and nails that held me to the whipping post and that cruel rugged cross. My love held and fixed me there, even unto death.

My children, ponder, meditate upon these truths often. Let them permeate your soul. Try to fathom my true love toward you. Understand that even in your own suffering, I am always with you. I will never fail or forsake you. I understand your pain in ways you could never fathom. I may be silent but I will never leave your side and I am always there, weeping as you weep.

Remember, always my child, my great love for you and all that I endured just for you. Let this truth melt your stone heart into a heart of flesh."

Prayer

My dear sweet, precious love Jesus.
Please help my hard and wicked heart,
To accept your sacrifice of love toward me.
Help me to comprehend the depths, the hight and width, of your great love toward me.
Please help me in my weakness and be kind and merciful toward me.
In Jesus name I ask,
Amen.

10. We must recognise the great love our Lord Jesus Christ has toward us.

❖

"Oh my sweet and beautiful friend, my God, my saviour, my redeemer, Jesus Christ my Lord and king. I thank you dearly that no height and no depth, has stopped your love toward me. There are no chains that restrict you except the bonds of love that you have toward me. Your love is so great and so pure, you endured so much pain for me that I may be spared from such punishments which you bore.

You are my love and my champion, my friend, my king and my God. Oh how my heart aches with love and gratefulness toward you. I am so diseased with the mystery of sin that resides in every fibre of my being. There is no good health within except that which you give, through the wondrous power of your atoning blood. Your blood, Your precious and beautiful blood which was spilled for me, to set me free from the cancer of sin.

   Your blood is so pure, that as it ran down that old rugged cross and seeped into the mud, the ground ripped open, understanding that it was not worthy of such a sacred thing.

   Oh my Lord, how can I truly speak of things which I can barely understand? Your flesh and your blood was given to me, to set me free from the power of sin and death. Your blood is the joy of my heart as I drink from that ancient fountain. Without the precious blood of Jesus how could I ever come into the presence of my Holy Love? Why you would endure such agonies on the cross for me is beyond my comprehension.

   Ah, my lovely, beautiful Jesus, my Lord and God, it greatly pleased you to go to the whipping post for me. It greatly pleased you to carry my cross and become nailed to it. You became accursed for me, beaten and broken for me. You allowed Yourself to be put to death for me. You placed yourself upon the altar of God and allowed the Father to offer you up in my place.

   Oh how the heavenly Father was angered by my many, many sins, my desertion and my wickedness. Yet my loving Father sent you, His only Son, to be an acceptable substitute for me. You my Lord Jesus, died in my place. You took such a beating and endured such pain, all the while you received it with patience because of Your love for me. Truly, truly, what kind of love is this?

Christ, You know my weakness and fragility, you know that I am mortal and weak of frame. I am forever thankful for your kindness and the pity You have toward me. I am so thankful yet sorrowfully pained to know you became a human shield for me. You took on your flesh the bloody beating that I deserved. Your flesh was whipped, lashed, split and torn. You were struck with awful blows, one after another. You were cruelly mutilated in the service of my defence.

Because of Your great love, you endured such torment and abuse to pay the heavy penalty for my wickedness and sins. Because of what you endured you have completely reconciled me to my loving heavenly Father. No one else but you, my sweet Jesus, could have permitted and enabled this wonderful blessing.

You have given me joy and sweet life in abundance. I do not deserve this happiness but I am forever grateful that you did this for me. Oh my Jesus, the ancients of the faith called this sacrificial love, 'The Passion.' Could it be called anything else? No, indeed it could not."

Prayer

Oh my sweet fragrant Jesus.
My words could never truly convey my gratitude toward you.
I am so grateful that you went to the cross for me.
I am so grateful that you made a way for me to be at peace with the Father.
Thank you for the blood, thank you for the eternal life you have given me.
May I always be thankful each and every day for your costly sacrifice for me.
I love you.

Amen.

11. By the authority of the blessed Trinity, all grace and kindness comes from Him.

❖

"My sweet Jesus, my love, my Redeemer and honoured friend, you have done so much for me and blessed me beyond measure. You have blessed me with every heavenly blessing.[55] You have given me joy and peace with the heavenly Father.[56] You became sin for me that I might become the righteousness of God.[57] Even now in the

---

[55] Ephesians 1:3

[56] Romans 5:1

[57] 2 Corinthians 5:21

heavens you are a high priest for me, making intercessions to the Father on my behalf.

My heart wants to cry with great tears of thankfulness for what you have done for me on that old rugged cross. I am so grateful for your love and kindness toward me. Truly my cup runneth over because of your great love.

Oh, everyday I sin, everyday I make mistakes, so many mistakes my Lord. You have every right in your just and holy ways to condemn me and you would be wholly right and just to do so. Yet you do not. Your blood covers my sins and everyday your kindness is new with every morning. Your grace is so great toward me, I am humbled by your love my Lord.

Lord, I have so little to offer up to you, I seem to only present to you my short fallings and sins every day. Yet my sins you take from me and separate them from me, as far as the east is from the west.[58] I can only offer myself to you as a love offering, my Lord. Even though I fail and make mistakes, I want to daily lay down my life for you as you once did for me.

I am reminded every day that everything comes from you, that I live and have my being in you. You lavish mankind with gifts of natural beauty, spiritual beauty, eloquence, riches, temporal and spiritual blessings, they all come from you. I have nothing in myself that I can boast of. All that I am is from you, through you and by you. The

---

[58] Psalm 103:12-14.

fact that I wake every morning and breath air is because of your grace and kindness toward me.

Prayer

Lord, I implore thee, may I never become foolish and take pride in the very gifts you have given me.
May I not be like the fool who thinks in his heart, "There is no God."
May I never live a moment where I forget you.
Help me in my weakness God, to always be aware of your presence and kindness toward me everyday.
May I live everyday in fulness for you, my sweet Lord.
May my life be a fragrant offering to you.
May my life be a living prayer of gratitude toward you.
In Jesus Name.
Amen.

12. How one might anger the Lord by being unkind toward the poor.

❖

'He who gives to the poor will not want, but he who hides his eyes will get many a curse.'[59]

"Oh my sweet precious love and saviour, Jesus Christ. My most loving and kind and generous Lord and God. I understand that I break your commandments every day of my life. I have transgressed your heart and the ways of your kingdom. You have blessed me with such fortunes of which you have made me a keeper, yet I have not been faithful in always giving to those who really are in need.

I have often seen the poor and walked by, pretending that I am not aware of their plight and poverty. I have

---

[59] Proverbs 28:27 RSV

justified why I should ignore them through self righteous judgements and assumptions. Through my cruel judgements and assumptions, I have become the meanest of pharisees. I bear religion but lack its heart. I have the form of religion but deny its power, the power of love and compassion.

Even when I do give to the poor, it is always a minimum. I may give them some short change, whilst I spend much money on trinkets and baubles for myself. I have often worn myself out with my evil behaviour. I have vexed my soul and worse of all, grieved your Holy Spirit with my hardness of heart.

My hardness of heart only proves my ingratitude toward you and your grace. Have you not said my Lord, "Freely you have received, now freely give?"[60] My Lord, my sweet beloved, please forgive my hard and callous heart. Please let me love people as you love people. Please let me be kind and generous as you are kind and generous.

Lord, please forgive me when I sleep well in my warm bed, giving no thought to those whom I know are suffering and groaning under the weight of poverty. Each day my Lord, you send me wonderful blessings, each day my cupboards are well supplied and I have everything I need.

Sadly I have taken your gifts and blessings and have merely hoarded them up for myself and my own personal comfort and pleasure. I have ignored the plight of my

---

[60] Matthew 10:8

brothers and sisters because of my own wicked and selfish heart.

I am a very wicked sinner, a man wrapped in selfish ways and selfish pleasures. For what reason did you bless me Lord? So that I could just gorge myself on personal wealth? Or that I could be your agent of providence to those around me?

Oh sweet Jesus, I beg your forgiveness. Instead of walking in the paths of righteousness and walking in your statutes and ordinances, I have instead walked the many pathways to satiating the desires of my flesh. I have pleased myself in this world and furnished my body with all the pleasures and entertainment this world offers. Please forgive me my precious Jesus."

Prayer

Oh my beloved Jesus.
Please, please forgive me
I have become hard hearted and forgetful of the poor and the needy.
Please help me to be more generous with my time, money and gifts.
Please help me to be generous as you are generous.
Please help me to be kind as you are kind.
Please help me to love as you love.
Please help my weak and sinful heart.
That I may show your kindness and your love to all, and that I no longer turn a blind eye to those in need.
I am forever in your debt my lord.

Amen

13. No person should counterfeit more beauty than nature permitted.

❖

Saint Benedict wrote a book back in 516 AD, entitled, 'The Rule.' This was about the way of life for monks and nuns and how to order their religious life. Part of his book dealt with the famous, 'ladder of humility.' On this ladder are twelve rungs that must be observed to help one learn humility by example and life style.

Humility is greatly encouraged in the scriptures and it would behove us well to apply humility to our lives. Humility is such an essential ingredient to living a pious and godly life in our abbey of the Holy Ghost. Without humility we are poor and wretched in the life of the Kingdom of God.

'If the peak of our endeavour, then, is to achieve profound humility, if we are eager to be raised to that heavenly hight, to *which we can climb only through humility during our present life, then let us make for ourselves a ladder like the one which Jacob saw in his dream. On that ladder angels of God were shown to him going up and down in a constant exchange that we need to establish in our own lives, but with this difference for us: our proud attempts at upward climbing will really bring us down, whereas to step downwards in humility is the way to lift our spirit up towards God.'* [61]

Part of our humility today is how we present ourselves. We must always live our lives from a place of authenticity. It is important that we don't project ourselves to be something we clearly are not. Our security and significance comes from who we are in Christ, not in how we look or how we feel.

It is important that we do not cause others to sin by how we dress. For men and women to be scantily clad is not kind to others who may struggle with high levels of sexuality. Some may argue that it is the people who struggle that should deal with their issues, not the one wearing inappropriate clothing. Whilst that may be true, it is equally right and proper to not cause our brothers and sisters to sin. This was the Apostle Paul's argument in Romans Chapter Fourteen. Some believers had an issue of conscience with eating meat offered to idols, whilst others didn't. Paul stated that we should not use our freedoms in Christ to cause others to stumble. To cause others to stumble by our lack of modesty is both selfish and unkind.

---

[61] Chapter 7 paragraph two of St Benedict's Rule

"Oh my dear sweet Jesus, how we have lived a life of so many vanities. How we are so obsessed with our external appearance and how the world around perceives us.

It is one thing to be clean and tidy, but another when we cover ourselves in rich clothes and ornate colours. For what reasons and motivations are we doing what we do sweet Jesus?

Lord, the scriptures teach us that true godly beauty comes from within, not garments, ornaments, baubles and trinkets."

'Let not yours be the outward adorning with braiding of hair, decoration of gold, and wearing of robes, but let it be the hidden person of the heart with the imperishable jewel of a gentle and quiet spirit, which in God's sight is very precious.' [62]

"Oh gentle Jesus, you never went around parading in lavish clothes, you never tried to impress man. Rather you lived a simple, humble and wonderful life. A true life of authenticity to your Father, God. Your true beauty didn't come from your outer adornments, rather it came from your heart and your Spirit.

Oh sweet Jesus, please forgive me if I have dressed in a manner that caused others to stumble in their most holy faith. If my apparel caused others to sin in word, thought and deed. God I beg for your forgiveness if my appearance has led unbelievers to sin and added more fire upon them

---

[62] 1 Peter 3:3-4. RSV

in judgement. Please forgive my selfishness and worldliness.

Lord forgive me if I have made people think something of me that I am not by how I dress, the vehicle I drive, the trinkets and baubles I own. Forgive me for when I have used such things to change peoples perception of me. Forgive my counterfeit and lies to the world, oh my precious saviour.

Oh Lord how I hate the fake and vain ways of this world, yet still so often I find myself playing its games. I forget that I am of a different kingdom, I am of a new order, a new creation. Forgive me for being so utterly shallow, fake and carnal to the world around me.

Instead of shining the gentle humility and beauty of Christ, I have often lied to the world by trying to look younger than I really am, appearing to be richer and more successful than I really am. Oh God, please forgive my wretched and worldly ways."

How can I truly live in my abbey of the Holy Ghost if I have not detached myself from this way of living? You have called me to be a living sacrifice, to take up my cross daily for your sake. The ascetic life will never be mine if I continue to walk in the ways of the world, in the ways of the pride of the eyes and the flesh.

Prayer

Oh my dear Lord and precious Saviour.
Please forgive my worldly and fleshly ways.
Please let my life in you become beautiful and authentic.
Let me know you and love you in the beauty of Holiness.
Let my life be lived in piety and simplicity.
Help me to stop pretending to the world around.
Help me to stop needing affirmation from the world around me.
Help me to know that all my identity and reality comes from You and within Your beautiful church.
Please melt me, mould me, shape me into something simple and beautiful in Your eyes.
I ask this in your most blessed and precious Name.
Jesus.

Amen.

14. The way of self examination, sufferings and praises.

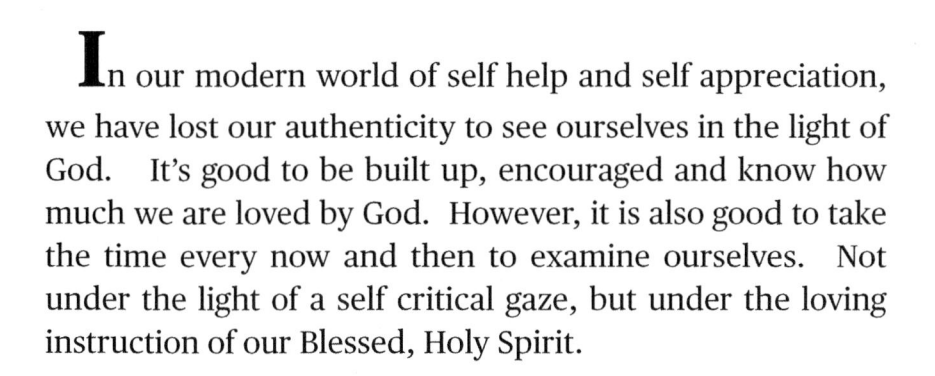

❖

In our modern world of self help and self appreciation, we have lost our authenticity to see ourselves in the light of God. It's good to be built up, encouraged and know how much we are loved by God. However, it is also good to take the time every now and then to examine ourselves. Not under the light of a self critical gaze, but under the loving instruction of our Blessed, Holy Spirit.

In today's Christianity such self examination is almost anathema. It's just something we must never do. Yet who told us this? Does the bible teach this? Is there joy, hope and strength in self examination with the Holy Spirit's lamp and guidance? I do believe there is.

Let's take a moment to see what the scriptures say about self examination and why it's necessary for a healthy, spiritual life in God.

'Let us examine our path, let us ponder it and return to Yahweh.' Lamentations 3:40 (JB)

'Examine yourselves, and only then eat of the bread and drink of the cup.' 1 Corinthians 11:28 (NRSV)

'Search me, O God, and know my heart; test me and know my thoughts. See if there is any wicked way in me, and lead me in the way everlasting.' Psalm 139:23-24 (NRSV)

'Examine yourselves to see whether you are living in the faith. Test yourselves. Do you not realise that Jesus Christ is in you?...' 2 Corinthians 13:5. (NRSV)

It is important for us in our abbey of the Holy Ghost to have a balanced soul. A soul that is not burdened with sin and shame, a soul that understands the power of Christ's forgiveness of sins and a soul who understands where it is at with God. It is important to allow the gaze of the Holy Spirit, to search our spirit and show us things both good and bad that we may need to understand, to help us become ever more Christlike.

How can we remove splinters from others if we are unaware of the logs that protrude from our selves? How can we truly know our progress in God, if we don't take a true and honest look at ourselves from time to time? No one likes to be seen as they really are, it is frightening and unnerving. This is why we must always self examine through the light of the Holy Spirit. If we allow Him and ask Him to show us, He will reveal those things that we may need to repent of and character traits that need addressing. He may also point out good parts of our personality that we had not previously considered. The Holy Spirit will never crush us or discourage us. He always wants the best for us and He wants us to bear the image of Christ. This is so important we understand this, as self examination and repentance can be so beneficial for our souls.

"Oh my sweet Jesus, give me a love for you and a hatred of sin. Not a hatred that causes me to judge others, but sees clearly the sins in my own life. Let me know how I grieve my love, the Blessed Holy Spirit, in word, thought and deed. Search me and know me and let me see clearly. Help me to understand that I stand in your beauty and in your righteousness[63]. Let me truly know that I am saved by faith and works of righteousness.[64]

Let me look into the abyss of my nature and see my sinfulness for what it is, give me a hatred for sin so that I may not sin against You, my beautiful Jesus. Give me strength each day to abhor those sins that break your heart and help me to walk in holiness and obedience to you. For Jesus, you taught us that if we love You, we will obey You.[65]

---

[63] See 2 Corinthians 5:21

[64] We are born again by faith in Jesus Christ, then we have good works to perform which validates our salvation, aids in our sanctification and gives us eternal rewards. See James 2:24

[65] John 14:15

I know that sin hardens my heart and separates me from God.[66] Help me Holy Spirit, to sin less day by day that my heart may appreciate and bathe in the love that Christ has for me.

Lord, when you walked the earth you stripped yourself of your glory, power and majesty. You became poor, afflicted and a man acquainted with sorrows. Yet, how is it that I always want riches, honour and recognition? Forgive me Jesus for my shallow and carnal ways. Help me to walk deeper into the path of the way of the Spirit, the ways of the Kingdom of God.

Please forgive me Jesus for asking and wanting things which you Yourself did not have, by demanding honour, trinkets and baubles, wealth, prestige and glory. Teach me to live life as you lived, for you learned obedience through suffering.[67]

As You are, so are we in this world, for we are Your body. The lessons You learned and taught us sweet Jesus, is the school master and the way of the abbey of the Holy Ghost. Understanding the psalter of our conscience, sins and shortcomings will enable us to live a life of joy and humility in Your grace, O Lord. For without You and Your grace, we are nothing.

We then must learn to praise you Jesus, everyday as we learn to appreciate, ponder and reflect upon Your grace

---

[66] Isaiah 59:2

[67] Hebrews 5:8

and kindness to us. For you have blessed us with every spiritual blessing in heavenly places.[68]

Thank you Jesus, for being the Sovereign of this holy sacred abbey. Help us to live this wonderful religion, in love, obedience and simplicity."

Prayer

Dear Lord Jesus, my sweet and precious Saviour.
Help me to examine myself from time to time.
Please illumine my conscience by your Blessed Holy Spirit.
Let Him and Him alone show me my errors and faults.
Let Him lead me and guide me so that I may learn to worship you in the beauty of holiness.
Help me to walk the path of humility, simplicity and holiness.
Let my life be a living sacrifice, a sweet savour to the Father.

Amen.

---

[68] Ephesians 1:3

15. climb the mountain of tranquility

❖

'*A tranquil heart gives life to the flesh...*'[69]

'And that peace of God, which is so much greater than we can understand will guard your hearts and your thoughts, in Christ Jesus.'[70]

Dearest saint, we must endeavour to live our lives in the constant peace and tranquility of Christ. He has given us sweet rest in Him. God has given to us the peace which passes all understanding. As the letter to the Hebrews states, we must contend to stay in that place of peace and rest.[71]

---

[69] Proverbs 14:30. ESV

[70] Philippians 4:7 JB

[71] Hebrews 4:11

Like all the great disciplines of the Christian faith, one must start slowly and place one step before the other. Climbing the mountain of tranquility takes time, devotion and practice. To learn to live in the place of tranquility and the peace of God is no easy task. Many of us have tasted of its fruit from time to time, yet there is a place, where we can constantly sit under the shade of its rest.

When king Nebuchadnezzar had Daniel, Shadrach, Meshach and Abednego ruling over the kingdom of Babylon, the country was ruled and guided by peace, consolation and tranquility. God used these four men to bring joy, peace, charity and humility to the land.

To truly live from the wellsprings of tranquility one must learn to drink from it through faith. Sometimes we don't have all the answers that we desperately want and need to know. Sometimes we don't have enough understanding to stay in a place of natural peace. However, God's peace is supernatural, and so by faith we have to trust that God is in control, even when our worlds are spinning apart.

God's tranquility makes no sense to the world around, but to the pious it is the nectar of eternal life itself. Jesus came to give us life and life in abundance.[72] Living in fear and worry is not the way of the kingdom of heaven. Fear, anxiousness, doubt and worry is a perversion of faith. Fear is when we place our trust in circumstances to cause us harm, instead of trusting God, who is mighty and able to save.

---

[72] John 10:10

Let's not live in fear, worry and doubt, rather let us drink deep, via the goblet of faith, the sweet river of tranquility, the still and quiet waters of the river of delights.

Prayer

Oh Sweet and precious Jesus.
Help me to live daily in your rest and peace.
Teach me how to live in your tranquility by faith, day by day.
Forgive me for my fears and doubts,
Teach me to ever trust Thee and in Thy goodness.

Amen

16. The duties of Discretion, Praise, Devotion and Penitence in our abbey of the Holy Ghost.

❖

Every abbey needs needs a treasurer[73], the treasurer for our abbey is known as Lady Discretion. She makes sure everything runs as it should, that there is balance and order. Discretion is an important virtue for the Christian to possess.

Discretion is the quality of being discreet in respect to one's own actions, thoughts and speech. It is about having

---

[73] The Treasurer is responsible for the financial side of the abbey.

prudence and decorum. The Apostle Paul teaches us that one of the fruits of the Spirit is self control.[74] To have mastery over our mouths and then ultimately our thought life is one of the highest forms of spiritual discipline and shows the virtue of discretion and self control.

'For in many things we offend all. If any man offend not in word, the same is a perfect man, and also able to bridle the whole body.' James 3:2 (KJV)

'For the weapons of our warfare are not carnal, but mighty through God to the pulling down of strongholds; casting down imaginations, and every high thing that exalteth itself against the knowledge of God, and bringing into captivity every thought to the obedience of Christ.' 2 Corinthians 10:4-5 (KJV)

Lady Praise is our worship and song leader in the abbey. Day and night she is encouraging us all to sing unto the Lord our God. Praise is an essential ingredient to life in the abbey.   As the prayers of *'the hours,'* resound, it is important to note that much chanting and singing of the psalter is traditionally done at these hours. Praise, worship and adoration is not something we do when we feel like it, rather, it should be a daily discipline to praise God, whether we feel we want to, or not. God is always worthy to be praised. True piety comes when we push past the slothfulness of the flesh and render unto God that which should be done.

---

[74] Gal 5:22-23

'Giving thanks always for all things, in the name of our Lord Jesus Christ, to God and the Father.' Ephesians 5:20 (Douay-Rheims Bible.)

Jubilation, is the companion of Lady Praise. In times of praise to our God in singing and prayer, the heart will sometimes overflow with joy and jubilation. The scriptures teach us, our strength is our joy in the lord.[75] To have no joy in God is an unhealthy place to be. We all have days where we don't "Feel" like giving God our best but if we can push through, irrespective of our "feelings" then sometimes God will reward us with the oil of gladness which is His joy.

Indeed the progress of our prayer life must grow into a place of maturity, where we push beyond the senses of the flesh, into the senses of the soul and then to the spirit. We must learn to walk by faith and not our feelings when it comes to our prayer life in our abbey of the Holy Ghost. This is the path of maturity, to push past feelings into the depths of joyous prayer.

Lady Devotion is overseer of the cellar[76] in our abbey and she watches over all the stock that is used for the glory of God. It is important that we follow her piety and devotion to Jesus. She is constantly devoted to Him, constantly remembering His passion. Lady Devotion always has her eyes on her Lord and Master, who resides in heaven. Her

---

[75] Nehemiah 8:10

[76] The Cellar is a large room under the monastery where food and drink is stored.

eyes are always fixed upon Jesus, in longing and adoring love.

'To you have I lifted up my eyes, you who dwell in the heavens: my eyes, like the eyes of slaves on the hand of their lords.
Like the eyes of a servant on the hand of her mistress, so our eyes are on the Lord our God till he show us his mercy.'
Psalm 123:1-2 (NAB)

Lady Penitence[77] is overseer of all the cooking, she often drinks the tears of sorrow for sin and serves her food dry with contrition. She is not often given to eating overly much for she fasts often. Frequently you will find her confessing her sins to God and we would do well to follow her lead on this, for the scriptures commend it. In the Lord's prayer we are to daily ask our God and High Priest for forgiveness of our sins.[78] In the famous passage from 1 John 1:9 we are taught… *'If we confess our sins, he is faithful and just, to forgive us our sins, and to cleanse us from all iniquity.'*[79] In the original Greek text, the tense of the word, 'confess,' is a present tense. This means it's not a singular event, but a daily event. Our sins create a barrier between us and God, and what better way to keep our lives in God's care and covering shadow than by simple penitence throughout the day. What a sweet joy to know our

---

[77] Penitence is the action and feeling of showing sorrow and regret for sin and thus doing repentance.

[78] Matthew 6:12

[79] Douay-Rheims Version

Redeemer always cleanses us from our sins and gives us peace with God. Blessed be His sweet and wondrously beautiful Name.

Mademoiselle Temperance is the keeper of the cold room.[80] She is always a lady of moderation and will never allow those in the abbey to be given over to gluttony. She makes sure no one has too much to eat or drink. The way of the abbey of the Holy Ghost is about the spiritual, religious and pious life. This means we give attention to the mastery of the flesh by living from the place of our spirit. The ancient church fathers taught that temperance to the flesh is a needful habit to live by, to train ourselves unto godliness. Sow to the spirit and you will reap from the spirit, sow to the flesh and you will reap from the flesh. This is why Mademoiselle Temperance must be seen as a beautiful lady, she always has our best interest at heart. She wants us to enter the deep inner chambers of prayer, chambers that pampered flesh cannot enter.

Lady Sobriety[81] reads at the dinner table of the lives of the great church fathers and sings to us how those desert fathers overcame their flesh and learned to enter the deep places of prayer and revelation. Lady Sobriety is always teaching us to learn from others' examples, so that we too may reach new depths in our intimacy with Christ. Lady Sobriety would encourage us to read books such as the five volume set, 'The Philokalia,' and the writings of Saint

---

[80] Cold rooms are places where perishable food items are stored.

[81] Sobriety is an old word for being sober and serious.

Tereasa of Avila. It is important to be schooled by the masters of prayer if we are to make any headway ourselves into the journey of prayer. Only a fool walks blindly, but a wise man seeks counsel and guidance from those more skilled than himself, for that is humility.

Lady Pity is the keeper of pittance, she is kind and generous to the poor, the sick and the needy. She will visit the prisoner, clothe the naked, be kind to those who need help. We must never give ourselves over to hard heartedness. We must always watch Lady Pity closely and imitate her ways. To have this kind of love is true perfection and fulfils the Law of God.[82]

Lady Mercy is the almsgiver[83], she is so generous with what she has, that she has barely enough for herself. She understands that she is blessed to be a blessing. The scriptures teach, *"It is more blessed to give than it is to receive."*[84] Lady Mercy is always looking how she might help the poor in money and time, not for personal gain or benefit, rather she is living her faith and loving and giving as Christ did.

Madame Fortitude[85] is the porter who guards the cloister of the mind. She protects the ear, eye, heart and mouth

---

[82] Romans 13:10

[83] Almsgiving is the giving of money, food and clothing to the poor

[84] Acts 20:35

[85] Fortitude is courage in pain or adversity

gates from wickedness and evil. She takes every thought captive to the obedience of Christ, she girds up the loins of the mind to help it to stay strong in faith and in the truth. She stops us from being given over to the lies of the devil and helps us to submit to God and His teachings.

Lady Honesty is guard over the novices[86] in the abbey and teaches them the discipline of being honest and truthful. She makes sure that they never bend the truth, stretch the truth, or be economic with the truth. God is the Truth, the Life and the Way, we must be imitators of Him as dearly beloved children.[87] Honesty and truthfulness is so important to God that it is clearly listed in the ten commandments.[88]

Lady Courtesy also known as Lady Hospitality, is the main innkeeper of the abbey. Her job is to make sure all the guests to the abbey are well looked after and provided for. However lady Courtesy being a nun cannot spend time alone with the guests, so she must be accompanied by Lady Simplicity. These two are perfect companions to one another. One without the other is of little benefit, but together they make sure all are made welcome in an appropriate manner.

---

[86] The novice or novitiate is a monk or nun in a place of training for the religious order

[87] John 14:6 & Ephesians 5:1

[88] Exodus 20:16

Lady Reason is the purveyor[89], she sells and deals in particular goods. She makes sure she provides for those within and without the abbey, tending to peoples needs in ways that are above reproach.

Lady Loyalty is the overseer of the infirmary, she lives to serve the sick and needy. Her love for Jesus is such that she sees Jesus in every living person, for they are surely made in His image. As she serves the sick, she serves Jesus, as she cares for the weak, so she is caring for Jesus Himself. She lives her live ministering to Christ through the people she tends to, thus fulfilling the parable of the sheep and the goats from Matthew 25:33-46.

The fond companion of Lady Loyalty is Lady Largess.[90] She is so generous to the people Lady Loyalty cares for. No expense is spared to help the sick, poor and the needy. If medicine, clothes, food and shelter is what is required then Lady Largess will make sure it gets done. After all if we have done it to the brethren we have done it unto Jesus Himself.

'...I say to you, as long as you did it to one of these my least brethren, you did it to me.' Matthew 25:40. (Douay-Rheims)

Madame Meditation, she is a very wise and wonderful lady to know. She is the overseer of the granary and so provides good quality daily bread for all at the abbey. Lady

---

[89] A purveyor is one who sells and deals in particular goods.

[90] Largess means to be generous with gifts and money.

Meditation will cause us to have riches of revelation from the sacred scriptures.

King David very much loved Madame Meditation, he often wrote about her in his psalms.

'I remembered the days of old, I meditated on all thy works: I meditated upon the works of thy hands.' Psalm 142:5 (Douay Rheims)

The secret of seeing Jesus in the text of the scriptures and especially within the Torah, the Law of God, is to meditate upon the scriptures. Contemplate the law of God day and night as Psalm One instructs us. A good thought and revelation from meditation is much better than a wordy prayer.

Prayer is a wonderful thing, but it is a journey and a process. There are many rooms in prayer as there are many rooms in our spiritual abbey. There are degrees of prayer, depths of prayer, and differing kinds of prayer.

Life in the spiritual abbey is to prepare one's heart and spirit for a deeper spiritual walk with God which will in turn lead to a richer and deeper prayer walk with God. For understanding more on the way of prayer may I recommend, 'Interior Castles,' by Saint Teresa of Avila. Her book, like this one, explains how different rooms in a castle reveal degrees of prayer and intimacy with Christ Himself.

True and deep prayer is one where we say little before God, where words simply cannot convey what we feel. As the scriptures say, *'Be still and know that I am God.'*[91] It is this silent prayer where we meditate in the presence of God. This kind of contemplation is where we truly feed on the daily bread. Does not Jesus ask us to pray for our daily bread, indeed is it not super-substantial bread?

'Give us this day our supersubstantial bread.' Matthew 6:11 (Douay Rheims)

Jesus is the Word of God, He is our manna our bread from heaven. As we feast upon His word in meditation and prayer then we will be truly fed by the bread, as we do when we partake of the Eucharist.

Saint Augustine once said, *'Enter then, into your heart, and if you have faith you will find Christ there. There, he speaks to you. I the preacher must raise my voice, but he instructs you more effectively in silence.'*

Meditation and prayer go hand in hand. One should lead to the other and back again. This kind of prayer has a deep spiritual rhythm and beauty. It is probably the most intimate kind of prayer we can experience with God. However, it takes diligence, practise and effort to attain this kind of prayer. To sit still for long periods of time meditating in quiet prayer takes time to master. Remember always, start small and grow from where you start.

---

[91] Psalm 46:10

Prayer

Oh my lovely Jesus,
How I do so love thee with all my heart.
Please Lord I pray, teach me and lead me by your sweet Holy Spirit to pray.
May I learn how to plummet the depths and joys and difficulties of prayer.
Help me in my weakness, help me when I am strong.
Help me to know thee and love thee.

Amen.

17. Jesus promises abundance to those who serve Him well.

❖

In the book of Deuteronomy, chapter 28, verses 1-14, we are taught, if we love and serve the Lord well, He will bless us with an abundance of crops and prosperity. We understand that these blessings are an abundance of spiritual blessings which God has generously lavished upon us.

'Blessed be the God and Father of our Lord Jesus Christ, who hath blessed us with spiritual blessings in heavenly places, in Christ.' Ephesians 1:3 (Douay Rheims)

God wants to bless our lives with an abundance of wheat. This wheat and its abundance comes to us by contemplation of the life and death of Jesus and meditation upon His sacred scriptures. The wheat in the abbey is contemplation, the wine represents meditation. The more we pursue these disciplines and live by them, the greater the increase and measure of divine wheat and wine we may partake of.

Such spiritual disciplines are indeed true devotion to Christ of the highest calibre. You may wonder why contemplation and meditation are so important in the life of the pious? The reason is simple, contemplation and scriptural meditation are the two great disciplines that lead one into the very presence of God and thus union with Him. His Spirit of Wisdom and Revelation will impart glorious truths from the sacred scriptures that cannot be discerned via the carnal mind.

The way we can truly know God is through contemplation and meditation. Knowing God **IS** eternal life, as the scriptures testify.

*'And this is life eternal, that they might **know thee** the only true God, and Jesus Christ, whom thou hast sent.'* John 17:3 (KJV Emphasis added)

To understand God through simple knowledge of the bible and theology is good, but it is only head knowledge and doesn't go to the heart. To contemplate and meditate upon God and His Scriptures goes beyond the natural mind into the spiritual heart. It is here, and here alone that one can truly touch the Divine One. Yes, we need the truth and guidance of good doctrine, but God is to be worshiped in spirit as well as in truth.

'God is Spirit, and those who worship Him must worship in spirit and truth.' John 4:24 (NKJV)

An abundance of rich anointed oil comes into our lives from delighting ourselves in the Lord. The scriptures teach us that our strength in God comes from our joy in God.[92] He wants to fill us with the oil of gladness, the anointing of His presence, as we take joy and delight in our God. This oil is used to light the lamps in our abbey and give us light when the darkness comes. A heart that delights in God is comforted by God in times of heartache and distress.

God gives to us the gift of the blessed wheat of meditation. He gives to us the full bodied wine of Devotion, then God gives us His oil of Joy and the Spirit of Wisdom and Revelation.

A very wise lady who always makes sure we keep to the sacred hours of the day is known as Lady Jealousy. She awakes all those in the abbey that they may rise early to pray. She rings the bell throughout the day and calls us to pray the liturgy of the hours. She calls us to pray Matins, Lauds, Terce, Sext, None, Vespers and Compline. This ancient rhythm of prayer that has not only been prayed by the church for two thousand years but also practised by the Jews in ancient times in various and similar ways.

St Benedict called prayer, 'work.' It is indeed a noble and the most holy of works. To fulfil our mandate as a Royal Priesthood, it is right and fitting for us to come to the throne of grace boldly and lift up prayers, psalms, hymns and spiritual songs to our blessed King of Kings. It is good

---

[92] Nehemiah 8:10

for us to pray personal prayers to God, to meditate and contemplate. However, it is equally important to have fixed times in the day to raise up more formal prayers to God. These formal prayers in the form of liturgy and psalms are important because it leads us into the place of communion. When we pray the office of the hours we are joining many others in Christ's church all over the world praying the same prayers. This is where we are praying with the church, whereas personal prayers are prayers within the church. There is great power in a church that is praying the same prayers throughout all the earth.

Allow Lady Jealousy to have her work and way in your heart. Allow her to set your life to the ancient rhythm of prayer. Let her govern your life to a more God and prayer centric life style, where our lives revolve around the ancient times of daily prayer. Allow her to enable you to connect to the wider church in spirit and truth, to pray with brothers and sisters that you do not know or have never met. Join the communion of the saints and have sweet fellowship with Jesus knowing that you do so alone, but also not alone.

Those who have allowed Lady Jealousy to set and govern their hours have all agreed to a richer and more prayer centric life than they ever had before.

Prayer

Dear Lord God Almighty,
Teach me the ways of prayer, teach me to pray the hours of the day.
Teach me to meditate on your sacred scriptures,
Teach me to contemplate your life, death and resurrection.
Amen.

18. We must guard our hearts with all diligence in the love of our Lord.

❖

Oh dear Christian, how wonderfully blessed is the soul that learns not to be slothful or half asleep. We must be ever diligent and jealous for our God and growing in our love for Him, by seeking His face daily.

In the great sacred text of Canticles of Canticles,[93] we learn the great mysteries of sacred love and intimacy with the divine. It would behoove one well to meditate on such a book and discover its riches and secrets on intimacy with the living God. Canticle of Canticles teaches us the heart of intimacy, this is essential if we wish to live the pious religious life in our abbey of the Holy Ghost.

---

[93] AKA Song of Songs or Song of Solomon.

'Upon my bed at night I sought him whom my soul loves.'[94]

'Let him kiss me with the kisses of his mouth! For your love is better than wine.'[95]

'My beloved spake, and said unto me, Rise up, my love, my fair one and come away.'[96]

'...I found him whom my soul loves. I held him and would not let him go.'[97]

Can you see Christian, why this book is called the Canticles of Canticles? It is the song of all songs, the truest of love of all loves. It is a song about the bride and her bridegroom, it is a call for the church and her intended to come together in divine intimacy and communion. This is the heart of prayer, this should be the heart of everyone wishing to live in the abbey of the Holy Ghost. One must learn through love, discipline and obedience to diligently live life in this way. To do so will produce great and sweet spiritual fruits of joy.

Do not be under any false delusion, this way of life is not easy. There will be days you will soar the heights of prayer and times when you feel as though you are stuck in the

---

[94] Song of Songs 3:1 NRSV

[95] Song of Songs 1:2 NRSV

[96] Song of Songs 2:10 KJV

[97] Song of Songs 3:3. NRSV

mire. Wherever we find ourselves we can take comfort knowing that our God will never fail us or forsake us.[98] His blessed Holy Spirit is always there to gently nudge and encourage us on.

Remember it is the language of love that so easily sets the heart back in the direction of its intended. Always speak to God in the language of love and humility. Everything we do must come from the place of love. Set and fix your eyes upon Him and He will lead, guide and help you discover Him in your prayer room.

Prayer

Dearest Father in heaven.
Please help my hard heart to become a heart of flesh.
Please help me to love you more and more each day.
Let me never be cold hearted and formal with you.
Let me know you in true deep and reverent intimacy.

I ask this in the Name of Your Beloved Son,
Jesus Christ our Lord.
Amen

---

[98] Deuteronomy 31:6

19. Watch out for the evil sisters of Envy, Pride, Murmer and False Judgement.

❖

Dear Christian, beware the four sisters which Satan has placed into your abbey. They are the tares amongst the wheat of the goodness which God has wrought in the abbey of the Holy Ghost. Do not entertain them or give them any heed, for if you do, they will poison your soul with their wicked lies and deceptions.

The first of Satan's daughters is called Envy. She is a grotesque looking woman who is so cross eyed that she is incapable of seeing things as they really are. She will use many tactics to undermine those she is envious of.

The second daughter is Pride and Presumption. Oh please do not listen to this woman. She is always so proud of her own abilities and achievements. She looks down on everyone and is always making assumptions of others that is nearly always wrong. This woman is hunched backed with arrogant presumption and has a huge swollen chest full of pride. She is incapable of seeing herself as she really is. Never entertain her in your abbey, never eat with her or take pity on her. She is a foul serpent of a woman and a spawn of the flesh and the devil. Leave her well alone to her own self delusion and hypocrisy.

The third daughter is Murmer, she has such a terrible stammer, she is incapable of saying anything good about anybody. She is always causing gossip, strife and contention. She will undermine many to disrupt the love and unison of the community. She is ruthless, mean and cruel and cares not a wit for the body of Christ. She hates the church and like a venomous python, wants to infect it with her black venom.

The last daughter of Satan is False Judgement. This daughter is so lame that she is incapable of walking straight. She is always judging people, thinking herself to be better than others. She loves to bite down onto the unsuspecting with her false accusations and lies. She causes the Christian to lose their peace and question their own forgiveness from God. She is a wicked, foul and nasty woman. You would do well Christian, to stay away from these four women. For if you allow them, they will rob you blind, beat you to a pulp and maybe, just maybe they may succeed in murdering you altogether.

Prayer

Dear Lord Jesus,
Please I implore you,
Help me in my weaknesses,
Help me to not entertain envy, pride, gossip and judgment of others.
Please let my heart be pure and noble,
Help me to walk in the fruits of the Spirit and not the ways of the flesh.
Help me to love all people as though they were you in the flesh.
Oh help me I beseech thee,
My great and powerful Redeemer.

Amen.

20. It is by prayer that the four daughters of Satan will be removed from the abbey of the Holy Ghost.

❖

The four daughters of Satan will cause much damage to our blessed abbey of the Holy Ghost. There is no place for them for they will destroy all that is good and will tear down the walls of our dwelling.

In our abbey we must immediately notify our superiors and allow them to get to work on dealing with the foul mess which Satan has sowed. Madame Charity who is the abbess, Madame Wisdom the prioress, Madame Humility, the sub prioress and all the other good ladies in our abbey, will immediately get to work on dealing with those four evil women.

The answer to the problem is evident to the abbess, the prioress and the sub prioress; prayer is the answer to this conundrum. They tell all in the abbey that they must immediately go pray and beseech Jesus, implore and call out to the beautiful and majestic Holy Spirit, so that He may come in His beauty, power and grace to help us in our very great need.

Through prayers, worship and penance the Holy Spirit will come in His glory and throw out those wicked daughters of Satan. He will cast them out, those foul, filthy demonic harlots. Never again to be permitted back into such a holy and hallowed place as our beautiful abbey of the Holy Ghost.

Remember dear Christian, Satan is not one who likes to be defeated. He will again try to keep sneaking his harlot daughters in through back doors and open windows. Be diligent on this matter, he will always be sneaking around, always seeking to undermine your abbey. Be vigilant in your prayers, worship and pious life. Submit to God, resist the devil and he will flee from you in terror.[99] Pray, worship, love Jesus and repeat.

---

[99] James 4:7

Prayer

Oh my heavenly Father,
Please help me to see daily the wicked deeds of the enemy.
Please help me in my weakness to submit in humility to you each moment of each day.
Let Charity, Wisdom, and Humility guide me on the straight paths.
Lead me in the ways of righteousness for Your Name's sake.
Protect my heart, my abbey from Satan's foul attacks.
Let my life be filled with your glory.
In Jesus' Name.

Amen.

21. Conclusion to Returning to the abbey of the Holy Ghost.

❖

Your wonderful abbey of the Holy Ghost is now built and in good condition. You are ready to return to the ancient ways, the ancient paths and walk in a new and fresh way.

My prayer for you dear Christian, is that this book will not be merely a "nice" read for you, rather, this is a way of life; this is a devoted and disciplined life. Please know that it is through the disciplines as set down in this book that will lead you to a deeper and more spiritual walk with our beloved Jesus.

Listen to the voices of the good ladies afore mentioned throughout this book. In so doing, you will guard your hearts so that you will not transgress the rule of the ways of the abbey. Observe their ways and walk in them intently. To do so will be of tremendous blessing to you, even though it may be hard.

Always be diligent to not allow the four daughters of Satan to enter your heart. If they do, then hear the voice of Madame Discretion leading you to recover in prayer, through calling on Jesus to send the Holy Ghost to come and help you.

The Holy Ghost is our most welcome guest in the abbey and He will come as we pray and will come to remove the filth of the flesh and Satan from our lives. In so doing the abbey of our hearts will remain in a place of joyous peace and tranquility. The scriptures teach us that if we draw near to God and He will draw near to us.[100]   God is always willing and able to help us in the religious life of the abbey, but often or not we have to start with a bit of effort and time to draw close to God.   We do this through living according to the rule of the abbey as set down by the Abbess. We live a life of love, prayer and devotion to Jesus, whilst remembering to be charitable to all.

Finally dear Christian, this book is not intended to be read once and put back on the shelf. This is a devotional and instructional book, one which should be read often, from time to time. Maybe read a chapter a day, everyday, until you have engrained the teachings which lie herein. All abbeys throughout the world will daily read and study 'The Rule,' of their own order. So see this book as, 'The Rule,' for your spiritual abbey.

---

[100] James 4:8

Be blessed, be joyous, be courageous dear Christian and may you enjoy a more meaningful walk with God day by day in your abbey of the Holy Ghost.

Prayer

Dear Lord Jesus,
Please help me to live the rest of my days in this beautiful abbey you have for me in my heart.
Help me to live a life of more meaningful prayer and devotion to you.
Help me by the power of Your beautiful Holy Sprit, to keep the lusts of the flesh at bay day by day.
Protect me from the evil one,
And help me daily to keep my abbey in order so that it may glorify You.

Amen

Here ends the book entitled *Returning to the abbey of the Holy Ghost*.

Recommended Reading

❖

The Abbey of the Holy Ghost. Translated by Kathryn Anderson Hall, PhD

Sanctuary of the soul. Richard Foster

Celebration of Discipline. Richard Foster

Saint Benedict's Rule.

Journey into Divine Intimacy with St Teresa of Avila. Sr. Leslie Lund, ocdh

Interior Castle. St. Teresa of Avila

A Short and Easy Method of Prayer. Madame Guyon

Books by Chris Wickland

Basic Doctrine.

Hidden Gems of Torah.

The Blessing of Abraham.

Ten Biblical Steps to Freedom.

The Biblical Importance of Israel.

These books are available at Amazon in paperback and Kindle.

Podcasts by Chris Wickland

The audio teachings of Chris Wickland are available on all podcast platforms under the name of 'Storehouse 7 Ministries.'

The video teachings of Chris Wickland are available on YouTube under the channel name of 'Storehouse 7 Ministries.'

To contact Chris Wickland please email chris@lwcn.uk

Christopher Wickland came to faith in Christ in 1989. He currently lives on the South Coast of England with his wife Tracey and their five children. He is a Pastor, public speaker, author, musician and podcaster.

"Many of the wonderful spiritual treasures from earlier centuries have been missing from today's Christian reading lists. The result is that much Christian teaching today lacks spiritual depth and substance. This inevitably limits the scope of progress in the Christian life for many passionate believers.

Pastor Christopher Wickland loves the rich teachings of wisdom from earlier periods and traditions. This excellent book helps to redress the balance with his modernised update of the mediaeval prose text "The Abbey Of The Holy Ghost" from around 1350-1375. It is for the ordinary person seeking to live the spiritual life, based on monastic teaching. Each room in the abbey represents a Christian virtue or charitable act. You will be both awakened to, and encouraged by, the rich teaching in the pages of this book".

Printed in Great Britain
by Amazon